Working with Parents of Young People

Also edited by Debi Roker and John Coleman

Supporting Parents of Teenagers
A Handbook for Professionals
Edited by John Coleman and Debi Roker
ISBN-13: 978 1 85302 944 8   ISBN-10: 1 85302 944 0

of related interest

Supporting Parents
Messages from Research
David Quinton
Foreword by the Right Honourable Margaret Hodge, Minister for Children,
Young People and Families
ISBN-13: 978 1 84310 210 6   ISBN-10: 1 84310 210 2

Understanding 12–14-Year-Olds
Margot Waddell
ISBN-13: 978 1 84310 367 7   ISBN-10: 1 84310 367 2

Working with Anger and Young People
Nick Luxmoore
ISBN-13: 978 1 84310 466 7   ISBN-10: 1 84310 466 0

Listening to Young People in School, Youth Work
and Counselling
Nick Luxmoore
ISBN-13: 978 1 85302 909 7   ISBN-10: 1 85302 909 2

Enhancing the Well-being of Children and Families
through Effective Interventions
International Evidence for Practice
Edited by Colette McAuley, Peter J. Pecora and Wendy Rose
Foreword by Maria Eagle MP
ISBN-13: 978 1 84310 116 1   ISBN-10: 1 84310 116 5

Family Support as Reflective Practice
Edited by Pat Dolan, John Canavan and John Pinkerton
Foreword by Neil Thompson
ISBN-13: 978 1 84310 320 2   ISBN-10: 1 84310 320 6

Working with Parents of Young People

Research, Policy and Practice

Edited by Debi Roker
and John Coleman

Jessica Kingsley Publishers
London and Philadelphia

First published in 2007
by Jessica Kingsley Publishers
116 Pentonville Road
London N1 9JB, UK
and
400 Market Street, Suite 400
Philadelphia, PA 19106, USA

www.jkp.com

Library of Congress Cataloging in Publication Data
Working with parents of young people : research, policy, and practice / edited by Debi Roker and John Coleman.
p. cm.
Includes bibliographical references and index.
ISBN-13: 978-1-84310-420-9 (pbk.)
ISBN-10: 1-84310-420-2 (pbk.)
1. Parent and teenager--Great Britain. 2. Parenting--Great Britain. 3. Family services--Great Britain. I. Roker, Debi. II. Coleman, John.
HQ799.15.W68 2007
649'.125--dc22

2006029696

British Library Cataloguing in Publication Data
A CIP catalogue record for this book is available from the British Library

ISBN-13: 978 1 84310 420 9
ISBN-10: 1 84310 420 2

Printed and bound in Great Britain by
Athenaeum Press, Gateshead, Tyne and Wear

Contents

Part 3: New Ways of Working with Parents

Part 4: Conclusions

List of tables and boxes

Tables

Boxes

Preface

Over the last five years the Trust for the Study of Adolescence (TSA) has been engaged in a wide range of research in relation to the parenting of young people. TSA's projects have looked at the needs of parents and young people, at different means of providing support, at key issues such as monitoring and supervision, and at key transitions such as the move from primary to secondary school. This book tells the story of how these projects were developed, and the key lessons to be learnt from the findings. As always with the work of TSA, it has as its major focus the *implications* of research for policy and practice. TSA is committed to carrying out research that will be of relevance and value to those working in the field, and is also committed to the widest possible dissemination. The field of parenting is in a state of major change and development, and this book is our contribution to the continuing debate over how best to provide support for parents of young people.

Acknowledgements

Chapter 2

The authors would like to thank all the young people and parents who took part in the research. They are also very grateful to the Joseph Rowntree Foundation, which funded the research.

Chapter 3

The authors are very grateful to all the young people, parents/carers and practitioners who took part in this research. The study was funded by a grant from the Big Lottery Fund.

Chapter 4

The authors gratefully acknowledge all the parents who gave up their time to take part in the research described in this chapter. They would also like to thank the Alcohol and Education Research Council for funding the project.

Chapter 5

The authors are very grateful to all the parents who gave up their time to take part in this research. The research was funded by the Calouste Gulbenkian Foundation. The authors are very grateful for their support.

Chapter 6

The authors are grateful to all the project workers who gave up their time to participate in the research. The project was funded by a grant from the Tudor Trust.

Chapter 7

The authors would like to thank all the staff, students and parents at the two schools involved in the two projects described in this chapter, as well as the practitioners who worked with them. Both projects were supported by grants from a range of funders, including a social services department, the Carnegie

UK Trust and the Lloyds TSB Foundation. The authors are very grateful for their support.

Chapter 8

The authors are very grateful to the schools, parents, young people and practitioners who took part in the two projects described in this chapter. The projects were funded by the Home Office (Family Policy Unit, now part of the Department for Education and Skills) and the Carnegie UK Trust.

Chapter 9

The author is very grateful to all the parents who took part in this research, and to the workers in a range of organisations who helped to gain access to these parents. The research was funded by a grant from the Parenting Fund, administered by the Department for Education and Skills.

Chapter 10

The authors are grateful to all those who took part in this project, including parents, young people and practitioners. The project was funded by a grant from the Invest to Save bid.

Chapter 11

TSA is grateful to all the project workers, mentors and mentees for their assistance in the evaluation. The author is grateful to the Department for Education and Skills for a grant to undertake the research.

The Contributors

John Coleman is a psychologist who has a long-standing interest in parenting teenagers. He has written widely on this subject and is the co-author, with Debi Roker, of *Supporting Parents of Teenagers: a Handbook for Professionals*, also published by Jessica Kingsley Publishers. He founded TSA in 1989 and served as Director until he retired in 2005. He currently works as an independent consultant.

Lester Coleman is currently the Research Team Manager at TSA. Lester has been researching young people's health for the last 15 years, mainly in the areas of alcohol use, sexual health and sporting and physical health. His main interest is to ensure research findings have implications for policy and practice in relation to young people and parenting. He has previously worked at Exeter University, Southampton University, and the Open University.

Louise Cox is a researcher at TSA. She is currently working on a number of projects concerned with young people's health, including young people and the determinants of sport participation, and a project into parent–young people communication about alcohol. Louise has a BA in Developmental Psychology and an MSc in Health Psychology.

Kerry Devitt has been at TSA since April 2003, working across a range of projects primarily related to young people and education. Kerry has a background in psychological and social research, and has worked at both the University of Sussex and the University of Melbourne. Her main areas of interest are gender and society, gender and education, perceptions of ability in education and parenting styles.

Amanda Holt was a researcher at TSA until 2004. She worked on a range of projects relating to parenting, teenagers and family life. Prior to that she was a teacher and examiner of Psychology in Further Education. She is currently undertaking a PhD at the University of Brighton which is exploring the experiences of parents of teenagers who are involved in the youth justice system.

Cris Hoskin has 30 years of experience working with vulnerable young people and their families. She has worked as a special educational needs teacher, a specialist teacher in a young person's mental health centre and in a Youth Offending Team. Cris is particularly interested in working holistically with parents and their young people and in good quality training for parenting workers, focusing especially on the parents of adolescents.

Sarah Lindfield is the Project Leader responsible for TSA's parenting and youth justice work. Her background is in youth work, youth justice and family mediation. She is a qualified Social Worker with a special interest in positive conflict resolution and restorative justice. Sarah has an MPhil from Sheffield University which involved research into Community Justice Forums in Canada.

Kevin Lowe is currently Co-Director at TSA. Kevin has been involved in social care and work with young people for 25 years. He is particularly interested in how learning from a range of sources such as research and practice development can be disseminated in ways that are accessible for practitioners. He has written or edited a number of published training programmes.

Helen Richardson Foster was a researcher at TSA until 2003. She worked across a variety of projects in relation to young people, parenting and family life. Since leaving Helen has continued to work on a range of topics in relation to family life, for universities and independent research centres.

Debi Roker is currently Co-Director at TSA. Debi has been involved in applied youth and family research for over 20 years. She works across a range of areas, including parenting and family life, young people and health, youth social action and education and learning. Debi is particularly interested in how research can be used to help inform policy and practice. She has developed a range of materials based on TSA's research for practitioners, parents and policy-makers.

Julie Shepherd is a researcher at TSA and has been carrying out research with parents and young people for the last 10 years. Her particular areas of interest are support for parents and young people during the transition to secondary school. Julie is currently working on a DfES-funded project to support practitioners working with parents of 8–11-year-olds. Prior to joining TSA, Julie was a researcher at the University of East London. She has a degree in Social Science and an MA in Sociology, with special reference to qualitative research.

Nigel Sherriff has been a researcher at TSA since 2005. He has a broad range of research interests, including gender and education, masculinities, sexualities, social identity and intergroup relations, self-concept, transition to Higher Education and gendered subject choices. Previously he worked as a psychology lecturer and examiner in Yorkshire before completing a PhD in educational research at Lancaster University.

Stephanie Stace is a researcher at TSA. Whilst at TSA, she completed research into how monitoring and supervision is negotiated and practised in families. Stephanie is currently working on a project funded by the Big Lottery Fund, looking at how foster carers monitor, supervise and manage the behaviours of young people in their care. Before joining TSA, Stephanie carried out research into the educational achievements and life histories of young people in a young offenders institute, and on the experiences of students in higher education. She has a degree in Social Policy, an MSc in Social Research and a PhD in Education.

Part 1
Introduction

1 Working with parents of young people: setting the scene

John Coleman and Debi Roker

The parenting of young people is today one of the most controversial features of family life. For anyone interested or involved in work relating to parenting, it is apparent that since the early 1990s there have been the most remarkable changes. From being a topic that attracted little public interest, it has become a topic of concern and importance to everyone from the Prime Minister downwards. There is now a range of television programmes tackling questions about how best to parent young people, and in the public sphere there has been a variety of policy initiatives aimed at parenting of children and young people of all ages.

It is not entirely clear why this should be so. Is it because parenting in general has become a topic of greater interest? Is it that parenting young people poses a greater challenge to society today? Is it that, within the family, there is more concern about how to 'manage' or 'control' young people? Are young people seen as being at greater risk today? It is certainly true that much publicity has been given to the fact that British youth appear to drink more, to smoke more, and to have sex earlier than their counterparts in other parts of the European Union. There has also been a lot of discussion about the possible deterioration in the mental health of adolescents, and there seems little doubt that in the public mind there are serious questions about young people and how to deal with them.

Let us first consider what changes have taken place since the early 1990s. This may help us to understand some of the reasons for the increased attention being paid to the parenting of adolescents. First we explore changes that we think have been useful and beneficial. We then turn our attention to developments that we feel are less positive.

Changes since the early 1990s which have been beneficial

There has been a clear change in recent years in the level of awareness of the importance of parenting. Whilst there is still a long way to go, it is undoubtedly the case that more people are aware that parents of young people have an important role to play, than was the case in the early 1990s. When the Home Office issued the consultation paper *Supporting Families* in 1998 it seemed a daring thing to say that parents of young people mattered. The message then was that to ask for support or information should not be seen as a mark of failure, but of effective parenting. Today that message would hardly raise an eyebrow.

A greater understanding of the role of parents has been promoted by a variety of research reports and policy documents. One of the most influential was the report by Desforges and Abouchar (2003) showing the link between school attainment and parental involvement in homework and school activities. Another key document was the review, commissioned by the Home Office, entitled *What Works in Parenting Support?* (Moran, Ghate and Van der Merwe 2004; Moran and Ghate 2005). This publication represented an important landmark as it pulled together evidence on parenting support, and highlighted the lessons to be learnt from current research findings.

It is not easy to quantify the increased public awareness of the importance of parenting young people, and regrettably we have no research to substantiate the change in attitudes. Yet the very fact that governmental bodies have shown a willingness to review research and publish key findings speaks volumes, and of course the publication of key documents is not the only mark of heightened awareness. Another factor in the overall picture is the growth in voluntary sector organisations dedicated to supporting parents, and the interest many of these organisations have shown in the needs of parents of older children. The establishment of the National Family and Parenting Institute (NFPI), the work of Parenting UK, formerly Parenting Education and Support Forum (PESF), in relation to quality assurance and accreditation for parenting support workers, and the role of Parentline Plus in offering telephone support to thousands of parents, have all contributed to a growing awareness of parenting matters. This work has been matched by an extraordinary growth in the number of small charities dedicated to parenting support.

Turning now to government policy, two key policy initiatives should be mentioned here. In the first place the Children Act 2004 requires local authorities to publish a children and young people's plan. This has to be updated on an annual basis, and must include an element dedicated to parenting support. It remains to be seen how much of this focus is directed to parents of adolescents. The second example may be taken from the 2005 Green Paper on young people, *Youth Matters*, in which there is much about working with parents. Here we find statements such as: 'We want to ensure that parents of young people have better access to the information and advice they need...' (HM Government 2005, p.53), and 'Building on the experience of the youth justice system, we would like to see parenting support programmes become more widely available...' (p.53), and 'We would like to see opportunities for more parents to be involved in helping their children to make decisions about their learning and career choices...' (p.54). Clearly, as far as the government is concerned, parents of young people are central, and this is something that is very much to be welcomed.

It is not only the government that has been active in the arena of policy development. As will be well known to readers, since 1998 the government has invested hugely in services for families of the under-fives, services that have come under the rubric of Sure Start. In 2004 the policy think tank, the Institute of Public Policy Research, published a document in which it called for an initiative similar to Sure Start, but for parents of young people. The Institute proposed a new service, entitled Sure Progress, to offer a range of joined-up services for young people and their parents which would involve 'consistent support, intervention and activities'. As the authors wrote:

> There is a growing focus on providing support and advice for young children and their families, but there is also growing evidence that if you don't sustain that support, progress will be lost. Yet at the moment teenagers tend to get services more when they are in trouble with the police. (Edwards 2004, p.1)

A number of politicians and organisations came out in support of such an idea, again illustrating that the need for greater levels of support for families with older children is being more widely recognised than has been the case in the past.

To conclude this summary of positive changes that have occurred in recent years, it should be noted that applied and practice-oriented research has also played its part in raising awareness of the needs of parents of young people. It is certainly the case that some key funders, such as the Joseph Rowntree Foundation, the Calouste Gulbenkian Foundation, and the Lloyds TSB Foundation have all been proactive in supporting parenting research. The journal *Children and Society* dedicated an issue entirely to parenting and parenting support in 2005, and of the papers published, 50 per cent were concerned with the parenting of young people. Last, but certainly not least, the Trust for the Study of Adolescence (TSA) has been more active than most in carrying out research on parenting support for parents of teenagers. The results of some of these research projects are the subject of this book.

Changes since the early 1990s that have not been entirely beneficial

We now turn our attention to developments that we consider have been less helpful, in terms of supporting the parents of young people.

One of the most striking features of the public rhetoric concerning parents of young people has been the development of what can only be called a culture of blame. Countless newspaper articles and policy pronouncements place the responsibility for the behaviour of young people squarely on the shoulders of the parents. This message was exemplified by the introduction of the Parenting Order, a feature of the criminal justice system offering magistrates and judges the option of requiring parents to attend courses or counselling as a result, not of *their* behaviour, but of the behaviour of their sons or daughters. Parenting Orders were introduced first in the Crime and Disorder Act of 1998, and their use was extended in 2003 to include truancy and other educational misdemeanours. As many commentators have noted, there is something paradoxical about 'punishing' parents for a criminal act that is outside their control. The most extreme example of this was seen in the case of a mother who was sent to prison because of persistent truanting on the part of her daughter.

This legislation raises questions of central concern, in particular the nature of parent–child relationships (see Jones and Bell 2000). What do we mean by control? What is parental authority? How far can we expect parents to impose their will on an unruly or disobedient young person? What do we do with parents who are themselves overwhelmed by their health or personal circumstances? This dilemma is not easily resolved. There are undoubtedly cases where the requirement by a court for a parent to take greater responsibility for their teenager's welfare is beneficial. However, there are a much greater number of situations where it is apparent that a parent cannot reasonably be expected to have control over a young person, particularly where the young person does not respond to the imposition of normal limits and boundaries. Nothing is to be gained from the creation of a culture where blame is believed to be inappropriate, especially when that blame is laid at the door of those who care for our children.

The placing of responsibility with the parent has another difficulty associated with it. Such a concept is based on the presumption that the parent is the main socialising influence on the child. Thus the direction of influence is seen as being one way – from adult to child. This was the common assumption during much of the twentieth century, but in recent years there has been a greater recognition that things do not work quite like that. Socialisation is a two-way process, with the child being as influential as the adult. Thus the child's personality, communication skills and closeness to the parent will all play some part in determining how influential the parent can be (see for example, Stace and Roker 2004). We can see, therefore, that a culture which blames parents for their children's misdemeanours is using a faulty, dated view of how parent–child relationships operate. Once we acknowledge that the child or young person is a key player, not a passive recipient of their parents' values, we can begin to see that the concept of blame is flawed for scientific as well as for ethical reasons (James, Jencks and Prout 1998).

The conundrum of parental responsibility is linked to another contradiction in public policy, that concerning the rights of parents of young people. As has been noted above, where criminal behaviour of those under the age of 18 is concerned, parents can be held responsible by the courts. However, it may be argued that, at the same time as parental responsibilities have increased, their rights have been eroded. First, the *Gillick* case in 1986 established that young people under the age of 16 have the right to medical treatment (in this case contraceptive advice) without the knowledge and consent of their parents. This state of affairs has recently (January 2006) been tested again through a judicial review sought by a mother, Mrs Sue Axon, who was concerned that her daughter might be able to have an abortion without a parent being informed. The result of the judicial review was clear cut, the judge upholding the principles established by the House of Lords in the *Gillick* case some 20 years earlier. The judge stated that, so long as the young person is competent to make a decision about their health, and so long as the medical practitioner has tried to persuade the patient to inform their parents, then a young person has the right to confidential medical treatment. This includes having an abortion or any other type of treatment.

There is something very strange about a situation where a young woman can have an abortion without the parents being informed, and yet if that young woman throws a brick through a shop window an hour later the parents may be held responsible in court. How can we reconcile these positions? And what is the effect of such a contradictory situation? At present there is little we can do to bring the two positions together. We have two strands of thought, that of health and criminal justice, both appearing to be going in opposite directions as far as the rights and responsibilities of parents are concerned. In terms of the effect of the contradiction, it seems probable that it is another factor contributing to the general uncertainty and lack of confidence experienced by parents. Not only are they blamed for their children's bad behaviour, but their rights are being taken away at the same time.

It is perhaps appropriate here to make one or two further points about the situation of parents of young people. As we have seen, whilst some beneficial changes have occurred since the early 1990s, there have also been some shifts in policy and in public awareness that are less helpful. One example here relates to the role of fathers. Most people believe that there has been a major change in the way fathers are involved in child care today. However, closer examination shows that, with a few exceptions, almost all the focus in relation to fathering is on the early years. Very little attention has been directed towards the role of fathers of teenagers, and we have a very long way to go before there is any genuine debate and discussion about what fathering means in the context of adolescence.

Another factor that hinders the provision of support for parents of older children, is the difference in attitudes and ethos between primary and secondary school. Whilst there is much debate about how schools can support parents, and work more closely with them, again the great majority of such work occurs in the primary sector. With so much emphasis today on the concept of extended schools, there may be a real opportunity for parents of young people to have better relationships with secondary schools. Yet the evidence is not encouraging. For many parents of young people, schools are bewildering institutions, unlikely to offer the support and advice that is so badly needed.

In considering the changes since the early 1990s, a final comment must be devoted to the extraordinary paradox, that in Britain today most of the resources available for the support of parents of young people are coming through the criminal justice system. Of course such support is very welcome, even though it may come far too late for some families. However, it is a bizarre state of affairs when a parent can only get help once the young person becomes known to the police or the youth offending team. Not only is this an expensive way to deliver support, since clearly there is less possibility of change once this situation has been reached, but there is something contradictory to the principles of any welfare state that parental support and offending become linked in this way.

Support for the parents of young people

During the last few years there has been a greatly increased focus on the nature of support. What do parents want? How is it best to conceptualise this support? Perhaps most important, 'what works' in parenting support? It remains the case that much of the research that is available concerns itself with parents of younger children, and we still lack a substantive body of evidence concerning parents of adolescents. Nonetheless, there are some important lessons to be learnt from the research that has been carried out in recent years, and some brief mention of this is appropriate here.

In the first place there has been intense debate surrounding the different notions of support. One helpful analysis of the variety of models available can be found in Miller and Sambell (2003). These authors represent an approach which places particular emphasis on the importance of the parent's perspective in the development of support services. Following a series of focus groups with parents, the authors distinguished between three models, that apply in particular to groupwork settings – the dispensing model, the relating model and the reflecting model. The dispensing model is one that sees support as offering the parent a means of dealing with behaviour. Thus, any work with parents would offer practical suggestions for changing the child's behaviour, thereby implicitly espousing a model which sees the child as the problem. The second model, the relating model, sees support as being about helping the development of the parent. Here parenting support is seen as focusing on the needs of the parents and validating them in their role. The last model, that is described as the reflecting model, sees parenting support as offering the adult an opportunity to think through and come to a better understanding of the parent–child relationship. Here the implicit model is an interactionist one, with both parent and child being seen as playing a part in the parenting process.

Miller and Sambell's research found that parents valued all three models of support, but the one that was preferred in all groups was the dispensing model. There was often disappointment among parents if some element of this model did not feature in their support package. It was this that they expected more than any other model. However, the other models were also prominent, but interestingly the last of the three, the reflecting model, was the least commonly mentioned. Further, it really only occurred among parents who had already had some experience of groupwork.

These three models are important, in that they represent very different approaches to parenting support, as well as reflecting different notions of how parents and children relate to each other. There are, of course, implicit value systems involved here, and it may be that whilst many professionals are more in sympathy with the reflecting model, parents themselves prefer (or expect) the dispensing model. Readers may wish to keep in mind the distinction between models, and consider which models feature most prominently in the chapters that follow. We should add that this is not the only context in which models of intervention are important. In Chapter 10, Hoskin and Lindfield describe a project in which five different models of support were used as part of an intervention project. Interestingly the models in this particular project conform more closely to traditional treatment models, i.e. family therapy, group therapy and so on, rather than the three proposed by Miller and Sambell.

The important point to note here, however, is that in almost all situations where support is offered by one person to others, some model of human interaction will be implicit within the relationship. As has been noted, each model has attached to it a set of values, and there is no doubt that the more aware professionals are of the values that underpin their work, the more effective that work will be. In addition, of course, it is important to stress that groupwork settings and parenting courses are only one form of support for the parents of young people. There are many other forms of information and support available. Much of the research and literature, however, is based on an analysis of group-based parenting programmes. It is important to stress that 'parenting support' is much broader than this, and takes place between friends, between and within families, and in relation to publicly available and specialist services. Many of the chapters in this book look at some of these broader elements of support.

We now turn to another key feature of work to do with parents of young people, namely the debate centering around the question 'what works in parenting support?' As has been noted earlier in the chapter, an important meta-analysis was commissioned by the Home Office (Moran et al. 2004), and we will draw on this, as well as on other published papers, for our discussion here. We should first say that the great majority of studies which report evaluation of outcomes concern themselves with parents of younger children. Indeed in a recent paper (Reyno and McGrath 2006) describing the seminal studies identifying predictors of what was called 'parent training efficacy', not a single study referred to children over the age of ten. In the Moran et al. review, some reference was made to work with parents of adolescents, enabling the authors to conclude that 'early interventions report better and more durable outcomes for children, but late intervention is better than none, and may help parents deal with parenting under stress' (Moran et al., p.122).

In addition to this conclusion, the review advanced some further important suggestions about 'what works'. First it is argued that interventions with a strong theory base and a clearly articulated model of how behaviour change can be brought about are more likely to have good outcomes. Second, interventions that pay close attention to implementation factors, such as engaging parents and maintaining this engagement, are more likely to show positive effects. Third, the length of the intervention is important, with those continuing over time, particularly if they include booster sessions, or follow-up work, having positive outcomes. Last, staff training is seen as being critical to the development of effective interventions. Where staff were thoroughly trained, and already had substantive experience in work with parents, the intervention had a higher chance of being effective.

The Moran *et al.* (2004) review also identified some major questions for further consideration where parenting support in the UK is concerned. In the first place it is clear that there is a serious lack of high-quality evaluation of parenting support. As is the case in many areas of the social sciences, we appear unwilling to invest seriously in research on long-term outcomes of treatment programmes. Such a gap evidently hampers our search for answers to questions about what works. In addition to this difficulty, we remain uncertain about the link between a change in attitude and an alteration in problem behaviour. Thus, evaluations that look at process may show that parents feel better about themselves following a parenting course, but there remains a very wide gap between that conclusion and one that identifies ways to reduce a young person's challenging behaviour. Put another way: '…we still do not know how positive changes in a parent's knowledge and attitudes can be translated into changes at the behavioural level' (Moran *et al.* 2004, p.126).

In addition to this issue, many other questions remain to be answered. What is the comparative efficacy between group and individual interventions? What is the impact of involving young people directly in parenting interventions? How can we ensure that our interventions are sensitive to the attitudes and values of different cultural groups? In addition, what other forms of information and support are effective? We know very little about media campaigns, the use of leaflets and fliers, or about how informal and interpersonal support works in and between families.

It is essential also that the question of gender is not ignored. Parenting support remains very much an activity that involves mothers more than fathers, and nowhere is this more apparent than in the parenting of teenagers. How can we address this divide between parents, and involve fathers in a more realistic manner in our parenting support work? Some of these questions will be addressed in the course of this book. We can be certain that we still have much to learn where parents of adolescents are concerned, and some of the chapters in this book contribute to the continuing debate about what works in parenting support.

Conclusions

The purpose of this chapter has been to place the content of this book within the current context of parenting in the UK. As has been noted, parenting in general is much higher on the agenda than has been the case in previous decades. There is, however, a striking paradox about the parenting field. The focus of much of the academic work and practice development is concerned with the parenting of young children, yet the degree of anxiety, both public and political, is much higher when it comes to parenting young people. It is our wish to highlight this contradiction, and to encourage all who are concerned with parenting that there is a pressing need to pay greater attention to research and practice development relating to parents of young people.

This is especially the case because the very limited research we do have (for example, Allard 2003) shows clearly that parents of adolescents who do seek help have a very hard time of it. There is a serious lack of support services for this group of parents, apart from the interventions being offered through the youth justice system. As Allard (2003, p.40) says: 'It is clear from those interviewed for this report that many families (of teenagers) struggle to access support'. There are a number of reasons for this, including the fragmentation and limited resources of voluntary sector agencies, and the fact that statutory services are generally available only for situations of family breakdown or child protection. However, we should not forget that parents themselves are sometimes uncertain or ambivalent about seeking help. Allard puts it like this: 'It was clear from many parents interviewed that one of the factors that made it more difficult to ask for help was their own feeling that having to do so meant that they had failed as parents' (p.40).

This book aims to contribute to knowledge about ways and methods for supporting the parents of young people. It should be stressed at this point that we use a broad definition of the term 'parents', and when used in this book it refers to all those with a parenting role, including biological parents, step-parents, foster carers, grandparents, etc. The book addresses two key themes, which reflects this diversity. One has to do with *new research* about the parents of young people (Part 2), and the other is concerned with *new ways of working* with parents (Part 3). We believe that these two themes are complementary. New research, as, for example, studies of communication, or of monitoring and supervision, is an essential underpinning for the development of new approaches to support. Thus, the more we know about the way parents handle transitions, such as that from primary to secondary school, the better we are able to tailor support services to the needs of parents. We hope that the chapters in this book will offer something for all practitioners, as well as contributing to the debate about the nature of the parenting experience for young people in Britain today.

References

Allard, A. (2003) *The End of my Tether.* London: National Children's Homes.

Desforges, C. and Abouchar, A. (2003) *The Impact of Parental Involvement, Parental Support and Family Education on Pupil Achievements and Adjustment.* Research Report 443. London: Department for Education and Skills.

Edwards, L. (2004) *The Lever Faberge Family Report, 2004: Parenting under the Microscope.* London: Unilever and Institute of Public Policy Research.

Gillick v West (1986), Norfolk and Wisbech Area Health Authority, House of Lords.

HM Government (2005) *Youth Matters.* London: The Stationery Office.

Home Office (1998) *Supporting Families: A Consultation Paper.* Family Policy Unit Green Paper. London: Home Office.

James, A., Jenks, C. and Prout, A. (1998) *Theorizing Childhood.* London: Polity Press.

Jones, G. and Bell, R. (2000) *Balancing Acts: Youth, Parenting and Public Policy.* York: Joseph Rowntree Foundation.

Miller, S. and Sambell, K. (2003) 'What do parents feel they need? Implications of parents' perspectives for the facilitation of parenting programmes.' *Children and Society 17,* 1, 32–44.

Moran, P. and Ghate, D. (2005) 'The effectiveness of parenting support.' *Children and Society 19,* 4, 329–336.

Moran, P., Ghate, D. and Van der Merwe, A. (2004) *What Works in Parenting Support? A Review of the International Research Literature.* Research Report RR574. London: Department for Education and Skills.

Reyno, S. and McGrath, P. (2006) 'Predictors of parent training efficacy for child-externalising behaviour problems – a meta-analytic review.' *Journal of Child Psychology and Psychiatry 47,* 1, 99–111.

Stace, S. and Roker, D. (2004) *Monitoring and Supervision in 'Ordinary' Families.* London: National Children's Bureau.

Woodhead, M., James, A. and Thomas, N. (eds) (2005) 'Parenting and parent support.' *Children and Society 19,* 4, 261–342.

Part 2

New Research and Implications for Practice

2 How monitoring and supervision work in families: a study of 50 young people and their parents

Debi Roker and Stephanie Stace

The terms 'monitoring', 'supervision' and 'tracking' are used in a wide variety of contexts, by researchers, practitioners, policy-makers and parents. Monitoring and supervision are well-used phrases within policy and government discourse, particularly in areas such as youth justice, health and education. As explained in Chapter 1 of this volume, policy developments in all these areas have highlighted the relationship between young people and their parents/carers, and in particular parents' responsibility for the behaviour of their children (Coleman and Roker 2001; Gillies, Ribbens McCarthy and Holland 2001). The introduction of Parenting Orders in the youth justice field, for example, demonstrated the government's belief that parents should monitor, supervise and control their children, and ultimately be legally responsible for their children's behaviour. Similar developments have now taken place in relation to education, with parents now held legally responsible for their children's absence from school.

Despite the widespread use of these terms, however, remarkably little is known about how families actually manage this process. What do parents know about their children's whereabouts and activities? How do they obtain information, and in what ways do they use it? What do young people tell their parents about their whereabouts and activities? Are other people involved in this process? How do these processes vary by age, gender, locality, etc.? How, in general, is monitoring and supervision negotiated and contested within families? These were the areas addressed in the study on which this chapter is based.

Most of the research into monitoring and supervision has focused on particular families, mainly those experiencing difficulties or who are involved with statutory services. This study focused instead on 'ordinary' families, i.e. those who were not experiencing difficulties or involved with statutory bodies. The research was not designed to be prescriptive or evaluative, but instead to describe the processes involved. It was considered that understanding how parents experience monitoring and supervision could make a valuable contribution to work with parents and families.

Questions explored in the research

The following research questions were explored in the study:

- How do parents/carers and young people understand the concept of 'monitoring' and 'supervision'? How does monitoring and supervision work in practice?

- Does monitoring and supervision function in different ways in different areas of young people's lives, for example in relation to schooling and education, health and substances, or leisure activities?

- What is the role of the wider family and friendship group in monitoring and supervision? How are a young person's siblings, other family members, friends and friends' parents, involved in this process?

- How do issues of monitoring and supervision affect communication and negotiation within families? Are there key incidents or events that lead to monitoring being fundamentally changed?

- How are each of these aspects mediated and influenced by the gender, culture and ethnicity, social background and age of parents and young people, or by factors such as family structure?

Parents and young people involved in the research

Fifty families participated in the study, each family consisting of one young person aged 11–16 years, and one or both of their parents (depending on family composition). Participants were recruited via schools, youth centres, voluntary organisations and the Connexions service. The participants were drawn largely from two parts of England – the south-coast and the West Midlands.

Each parent and young person was separately interviewed, mainly in the family home. The interviews covered the main areas described in the research questions (listed above). In addition, each participant also completed a monitoring and supervision 'diary' over a seven-day period.

The families involved in the study were reasonably diverse. Both mothers and fathers were involved, and the families included two-parent families, lone-parent families, and step-families. The study also included those with a range of religious and cultural beliefs and backgrounds. In terms of social backgrounds, the participants were generally from more disadvantaged families.

Main findings from the research

The main findings from the research are presented under the following headings:

- how do parents get information about what their children are doing?
- trust and communication in monitoring and supervision
- monitoring and supervision of social life and friendships
- the wider support network
- how monitoring and supervision changes as young people get older
- gender in monitoring and supervision
- personality of individual children.

How do parents get information about what their children are doing?

Parents said that they got information in three main ways – by asking questions, managing young people's activities, and young people volunteering information.

First, parents said that they asked questions, in order to find out where their child was and what they were doing. Whilst none of the parents in our study said that they gained all of their knowledge in this way, many did ask their children directly about their plans. For example, as this young person explained it:

> They will only ask me if like, if I don't give them a proper answer... If my mum says, 'are you going to the park?' and I say 'yes', then she'll ask me 'who are you going with?' and 'have you got your phone?' and I'll say 'yes'. She just asks me questions like that. (male, 12 years)

In general, the young people did not feel that their parent/s were intrusive when they asked about their whereabouts and activities. Most of the young people understood that their parents were trying to keep them safe, and so were willing (most of the time) to provide them with information.

Second, parents said that they tried to manage their children's whereabouts and activities in various ways. All of the families felt that direct control *did* need to be exercised at times – for example saying that a young person could not go to a certain place at a certain time. This was usually seen as necessary when an activity might put a young person at risk in some way. Parents accepted, however, that most times arrangements needed to be negotiated and discussed. Most of the parents preferred to use the words 'boundaries' or 'guidelines' rather than rules. These terms were usually used for activities that were considered by parents to be non-negotiable – for example, times to be home, the completion of homework, and the use of certain internet sites. However, as young people became older, boundaries became more fluid and parents negotiated more with their child. For example, one young woman talked about how her parents negotiated with her about her activities and whereabouts:

> I have the usual time I have to be home in the evenings, and if it's any later then we have to like negotiate whatever's happening…there's no specific rules like I can't go here or I can't see this person…if I'm not sure if they'll like it then we'll just negotiate about it and I'll say, 'is it alright if I do this?' (female, 16 years)

A father similarly explained how monitoring and supervision worked with his daughter:

> I suppose there are lots of unwritten ones [rules], in terms of she knows the sort of people that we would prefer she was with. And just being sensible about being out at night or where she is going and what she is doing. And hopefully she has got lots of guidelines along the way as to what we approve of or don't approve of…I suppose those things have changed as she got older, so you start with narrow boundaries and then as she gets older you want her to know that the boundaries for herself can get wider, and she knows that she has to make judgements for herself about those and this is part of the process of growing up, that she understands and can make some decisions for herself. (father of female, 15 years)

Third, parents felt that they got information through young people volunteering information to them. For example, one young woman said:

> I always tell them where I'm going and I ask them first if I'm allowed to go and if not I just stay in…in case I'm not allowed to go there or if something's wrong down there, for instance, it's a rough area and I'm not allowed down there. So I ask my mum and if she says no, then no, and I just take it for an answer. (female, 12 years)

The information that parents wanted, and that provided by the young people, varied between the families. For example, some young people would have to tell their parents all the details about their whereabouts and activities, whilst others would only have to tell their parents where they were going and what time they would be home. The following quote highlights the vagueness of information that was sometimes shared between parents and young people:

> I do try to…I always tell them where I'm going…I don't give
> them the exact time…I'll probably say something like I'll be
> back about two perhaps and if I'm not back by two I phone
> them up just to tell them where I am and when I will be back.
> (male, 14 years)

A similar approach was highlighted by the mother of a 14-year-old
female:

> There are times when she will walk out the door without totally
> saying where she's going, and I had an example last Sunday. She
> had a phone call and it was her friend and she said we're going
> to the cinema… She left without totally confirming where she
> was going so she gives me sort of some idea but doesn't actually
> specify totally. (mother of female, 14 years)

The majority of the young people also felt they were able to withhold
some information from their parents, and that they had a right to do so.
There was a noticeable age difference in relation to this, with older young
people in the study having much more autonomy and privacy in their
lives. Generally, the older young people got, the less parents overtly
managed them.

Trust and communication in monitoring and supervision

A key theme that came out in the interviews was how monitoring and
supervision arrangements were seen as part of broader family relationships. Most parents considered that monitoring and supervision arrangements were not a simple set of rules or arrangements, but instead were
part of the broader relationship with their child. As one parent explained:

> I have noticed that a lot of other people monitor their children
> but don't actually communicate with them…a child can be
> monitored but learn nothing from it. You have to impart some
> kind of knowledge onto your children otherwise they don't
> learn right from wrong…you can't monitor your child properly
> unless you actually have a conversation and teach your child
> how important it is, how they should behave and shouldn't
> behave and to be a good example to them yourself. (mother of
> female, 13 years)

Many of the parents stressed that it was essential to communicate *why* there were certain rules or procedures in relation to monitoring and supervision. Young people too said that they wanted to understand why certain rules or arrangements were made. In turn, this made them more likely to be honest with their parents. As this parent explained:

> If we've been feeling worried about what she might be doing…we've sat down and talked about it…we negotiate what we think she should or shouldn't be doing in those areas…I do try and talk it all through and just keep on top of what the issues might be, and I might take her out for a coffee or something or a sit down…it's neutral ground and then she'll chat. (mother of female, 15 years)

Most of the parents also talked about the importance of compromise and negotiation. Parents usually only compromised with their children over issues they did not have very strong views about:

> I think as parents, especially in today's society…somewhere along the line you've got to compromise with them…if you treat your kids with respect and you're straight and honest with them…they're going to give you exactly what you give them…providing you know we can draw the line and say you don't overstep that and I don't overstep this, then fair enough. I think compromise is always a good thing. You've got to give them a lot of independence and trust in themselves. (father of male, 13 years)

Some of the parents also added, however, that sometimes they had to make a decision and stick to it, whether their child agreed or not. For example:

> I think most parents think their decision is absolute and they want their own way, no matter what. And negotiating with a child is probably quite alien to a lot of people and I think it is with myself…I find it very difficult really. I think if I've made a decision or I want the children to do something or not to do something I think I sort of put my foot down really. (father of male, 12 years)

This was a key finding in the study – agreements around monitoring and supervision were closely related to broader family relationships. Thus, the issues of how easily the young people felt they could talk to their parents, parent–child trust, and compromise, were closely interrelated. Next, however, we look at monitoring and supervision of social life and friendships.

Monitoring and supervision of social life and friendships

Social activities and friendships were monitored to varying degrees by all of the parents. The young people were aware that their parents had set rules or guidelines about their social activities, and monitoring was carried out in a number of ways in relation to this. These included parents:

- knowing where their child was, who they were with, and what they were doing

- agreeing times that they had to be home at night

- allowing less socialising on school nights, and more at weekends

- limiting how far they could go from the family home

- negotiating monitoring arrangements with other parents, especially those of their child's friends

- checking their child's whereabouts and well-being by calling them on their mobile phone, or the landline of where they were supposed to be

- limiting their child's activities in the winter months when it was darker, and allowing more freedom in the summer months when it was lighter

- monitoring their friendships, and discouraging relationships with other young people who parents believed were involved in risk-taking behaviours.

The above findings highlight the complexity of parental monitoring, and the number of guidelines, rules and expectations that parents used in relation to the young person's social life.

Many of the parents were worried about the effects that peer pressure could have on their child's behaviour. They were particularly concerned that their children did not get in with the 'wrong crowd'. As a result, most of the young people were not allowed to, or were discouraged from, 'hanging around' on the streets. Many of the parents, however, were aware that they could not control their child's friendships. As one father commented:

> Realistically there are certain kids I don't want him to go out with and there's certain kids I don't like. But I can't pick and choose who his friends are...I just say to him 'if there's any trouble, I don't want you involved in it'. (father of male, 12 years)

Monitoring young people's whereabouts, and who they spend time with, was closely related to the involvement of others in monitoring and supervision. This is explored next.

The wider support network

It was clear that many parents often relied on other people to either monitor their children for them, or provide an indirect form of monitoring through casual contact. Three main groups were involved: first, family members such as grandparents, siblings, aunts, uncles and partners of parents; second, other adults such as parents of the young person's friends, friends of parents and third, people in the community. These three groups are discussed in turn.

FAMILY MEMBERS

Most of the parents and young people felt that other family members were involved in monitoring and supervision to varying degrees. Parents stated that family members such as their own parents, and other children in the family, all helped them to monitor and supervise their child.

There were different ways in which parents felt other family members monitored their child. For example, some parents relied on family members, especially their own parents, to care for their child whilst they were at work or having to meet other commitments. One mother discussed how her mother and step-father monitor her daughter whilst she is in their care:

> She goes and stays down with my mum and step-dad...when they're there, they're responsible for the care and they have to live by the rules in that house, and they monitor their behaviour

there and what she's allowed to do…so mum does have the responsibility. (mother of female, 13 years)

About half of the young people interviewed also felt that their grandparents monitored them at certain times. This took place when they visited them, went on holiday with them, or when their parents were at work. For example:

My nan, loads of different ways… She asks me where I'm going, who am I going with, what they're like, where are we going, what's their name, things like that. (female, 12 years)

Another young person explained how she felt constantly watched and monitored by her grandparents:

My nan and granddad, I swear they watch me twenty-four seven without me knowing… Just usually check up on what I'm up to. Where I'm going, what I'm doing inside the house. In a way it's bad if you want to do something without them knowing. (female, 13 years)

Other children in the family, especially older siblings of the young person, were seen by many parents as involved in monitoring. One parent discussed how her eldest daughter helps her monitor her younger son:

She's in the last year of the same school…I don't know if it's called monitoring or grassing up really, I mean she'll definitely look out for him at school and she'll look out for him at home as well…if I'm not home from work she'll say well, 'where are you going?' and that type of thing. (mother of male, 11 years)

Many parents also said that their own siblings helped to monitor their children. This was by helping them with their homework, providing personal advice, or just 'keeping an eye on them'. One mother, for example, talked of how her whole family were involved in monitoring her daughter:

All of us keep an eye on both the children. Especially my sisters, they usually come and tell me 'she is not doing this right, and she seems to be doing this' or being cheeky, back chatting. Sometimes they ask me to talk to her, sometimes they shout at her themselves. I am quite happy that they tell her off. She is getting monitored by just about everybody, sometimes she gets quite fed up, we are all telling her what to do. (mother of female, 13 years)

Another mother described how her own family, and the family of her ex-husband, were all involved in monitoring her son:

Whoever he's with will [monitor him] because they all know he's got a tendency to get into trouble or to get out of hand so they will. So if he's round at my mum's and I'm not there, my brother or sister will be keeping an eye on him. If he's at his dad's and his dad's not there, his dad's brothers or sisters or his grandparents will keep an eye on him. (mother of male, 13 years)

A few young people felt that their fathers, who no longer lived with their mothers in the family home, monitored and supervised them whilst they were with them. As one young female said:

My dad does…I go to him and he just looks out for me and everything the same as my mum does. (female, 14 years)

Some of the parents and young people recognised that monitoring was carried out by family members not only in relation to their physical whereabouts and activities, but also in relation to their emotional well-being. One mother discussed how her own mother emotionally monitored her daughter:

My mum would in whatever way she can, she would say if she was worried about her and sometimes says to me, 'oh, have you found out what it is?' or something like that. Because if there's any problem with her or if mum thinks she's a bit funny she would want to find out about it, so she would ask me to find out or 'did I know?' or whatever. (mother of female, 15 years)

Young people recognised this and generally felt appreciative of receiving this from family members. A young female, for example, described how she felt looked after and monitored by her brother:

Like if I'm upset at school he'll come over to me and go, 'what's wrong with you, who's done something, what's been going on?', and then he'll go and have a go at them and say, 'what have you been messing with my sister for?'. (female, 13 years)

Emotional monitoring was seen as a caring act, one that makes sure that young people are being treated well and are coping with any personal difficulties. Many parents and young people talked about this emotional monitoring as much as monitoring of whereabouts and physical safety.

YOUNG PEOPLE'S FRIENDS' PARENTS AND PARENTS' FRIENDS

Many of the young people and parents discussed the role of either the young person's friends' parents, or the parents' friends, in monitoring and supervising the young person. The young people clearly saw themselves as monitored by their friends' parents if they were in their home, or by their parents' friends if they unexpectedly met them in their local area. Most of the young people considered that other adults who knew their parents would keep an eye on what they were doing. This might involve, for example, messages being passed to parents about young people's whereabouts and activities, or these individuals directly speaking to or monitoring what the young people were doing. For example, one mother said:

> I know a lot of the parents of the boys. I think if there was any problems or anything they would all sort of contact…if there was a problem, if I found out one of them had been bullied or something like that, then I would contact the parents, and I think they would do the same if they found out there was a problem with [son] that they thought I should know about, or you know, he's doing something that they think he shouldn't be doing. (mother of male, 13 years)

Many parents said that they preferred their child to socialise with children who were monitored in a similar way. This made the parents feel more secure, in the sense that they knew their children were safe and being looked after. For example, one father said:

> I think their [the friend's] mum does monitor and supervise when they're around in that area and when their children are round here we do the same…I think parents do if they know each other if they're close. I mean we're not close friends to the people round the corner but we know them in a way that, well we just know that we sort of monitor each others' children, it just goes without saying really, it's just a natural thing. (father of male, 12 years)

It was also clear that young people recognised that other parents monitored them when they were in their homes. As this 13-year-old explains it:

> If my mum and dad and their mum and dad have arranged for me to go around there then they would keep an eye on me. Because they know that my mum and dad have left me in their hands to look after me. So they would probably monitor me. (male, 13 years)

Many of the parents also described how they would try to find out more about the families that their children were visiting. They often wanted to meet the parent/s, visit their home and assess whether there were any risks for their children from involvement in the families. As these parents described it:

> I asked him loads of questions…what's his parents like…I was trying to get a picture of this boy…I've met his family and stuff and I met his father and mother. They said that he's not allowed to do certain things, and not allowed to go out…but it was important to me to know what the family background is. But I think definitely if they were closer, it would be a lot more, get to know the family a bit better. (mother of male, 12 years)

> We meet the parents, see what they're like, and that gives you a general idea of the environment that his friends are being brought up in. (father of male, 11 years)

In addition to family members, parents' friends, and parents of the young people's friends, people in the community and organisations were involved in monitoring and supervision. It is this that we turn to next.

PEOPLE IN THE COMMUNITY

Most families said that people in the wider community were involved in monitoring and supervision. Significant others such as school teachers, school counsellors, community group leaders and local neighbours were identified in particular by the families. These different individuals also often interacted – for example community leaders ran events in schools, and thus worked with school teachers to help monitor and supervise young people in activities. Many of the parents commented on how they have to leave their children in the care of others at times, and have to trust these individuals to look after and monitor their children. As this mother explained it:

> When she used to go to Scouts I handed the care over to the Scout leader and people like that. If she's off to judo lesson, the judo instructor. You have to try and make sure everybody's safe and police checked, don't you, but obviously any club you drop them at, you've got to trust that the people there are responsible for them and for that x amount of time. (mother of female, 13 years)

The above quote highlights the range of people who can be involved in monitoring, including school teachers, sports teachers and club leaders. For most of the families in the study, people outside the immediate family were identified as being involved in monitoring and supervision. Young people, as well as parents, acknowledged this fact. None of the families said that only parents and young people were involved, i.e. that the process took place in isolation.

How monitoring and supervision changes as young people get older

All parents stated that the age of their child had a direct influence on how they monitored them. Parents were aware that they monitor their child in relation to issues that are relevant to their age group. As one parent stated:

> Age makes an incredible difference, certainly to what you have to monitor...at 11 it's about roads and traffic and things like that...it's changed from that to being lured away by men...about being snatched or just grabbed as opposed to being persuaded...then it moves into all these other things...the sex, you get the drugs, you get the alcohol, and you get the relationships...and then of course, you know, like this year the school work would be high, very high. (mother of female, 15 years)

Parents and young people were aware of a number of changes in monitoring and supervision that occurred as young people became older. These included that young people could:

- go further distances from the family home unsupervised
- stay out later at night and go to bed later

- undertake more unsupervised activities with their friends

- have more responsibility and freedom

- be more involved in decision making, including negotiating with parents

- be treated as adults, with their parents beginning to 'let them go'

- be trusted more to make their own judgements

- have more privacy and time alone.

As these points show, a number of the changes in monitoring that occurred over time were related to the young person's whereabouts and activities. However, a significant number were also linked to the transitions through which young people become increasingly autonomous adults. Many parents and young people talked about how *change* in monitoring and supervision arrangements over time was essential, in order to help young people move towards independence. As one parent explained it:

> You have to grow with the age…it's a learning curve for a parent. I mean you start with this little baby that you've got to care for and gradually you've got to be able to release it into the world safely, but you hope that the influences that you have had on that child have prepared it to be sensible in the outside world. But it is difficult letting go. (mother of female, 14 years)

These findings support those of other studies, that also found an increase in independence, and a decrease in parental monitoring, between the ages of 11 and 16 years.

Gender in monitoring and supervision

In this study we looked at the gender of the young people, and whether that influenced the monitoring and supervision process. Most young males saw their gender as unrelated to how they were monitored, compared to some of the females who saw their gender as more significant. Many young women, however, felt that their parents monitored them more closely due to the risk of young women being attacked. These young women felt that boys were not as closely monitored, as they were less likely to be attacked or experience being abducted. However, not all the young women accepted this. As one young woman said:

> Girls are always portrayed as being the weak people that have to be kept an eye on more…we are going to be the ones that get abused in the streets…from complete random strangers, that we are more at risk. But boys get into fights and things. (female, 15 years)

Fewer parents thought that their child's gender influenced the way they were monitored and supervised. Most felt that young people had to be monitored in relation to risks to their safety, not their gender. However, a small number of parents did feel that the gender of their child affected how they monitored them, as they saw boys and girls as different. It was often said by parents that, for example, 'boys can look after themselves', or 'girls are more vulnerable than boys', and that parents have to be more protective of girls. One mother talked about the impact of gender on her relationship with her daughter:

> I do think you worry about girls more when they go out, getting pregnant, things like that. That's why I try and talk to her about things like that… I do look after her different to her dad. Her dad seems to think she's still six…you know, like a little girl. I realise now that she's 14, she's growing up. But I think her dad still thinks of her as his little baby…she'd rather be treated as a grown-up than, you know, as a little baby. (mother of female, 14 years)

This issue was closely linked to the personality of individual children, which we turn to next.

Personality of individual children

Most of the parents believed that the *personality* of the individual child was just as significant as their age or gender. Many parents reported 'tailoring' monitoring and supervision arrangements to suit each child's personality and maturity. Some young people were seen as more open and more honest, others as more vulnerable to getting involved in risk-taking. Parents said that they used this information to decide on the most appropriate monitoring and supervision arrangements for each of their children. As these parents said:

[What affects monitoring and supervision?] More the way she actually is herself, rather than the fact she's a girl, she's more of a shy, timid one than an outgoing confident one, so yeah, it's how she is. (mother of female, 11 years)

[Individual personality is important]…the trouble is, you see, my other children are slightly different from [daughter], they're different characters. [Daughter] is very quiet, she doesn't, doesn't really do anything, whereas my next one is more outgoing, so I think I'm going to have a few more problems with her because she's already into boys…two totally different people, and you do have to treat them differently…you do have to see what their personalities are like really, and how far they push you. They're all so different. (mother of female, 16 years)

I don't think it's age, I think it's mentality, I think you judge by the child, not by the age. (mother of female, 13 years)

It is of note, too, that many of the young people mentioned how their *parents'* personality had a role in how they were monitored and supervised. For example:

My mum watches over me like nearly every minute of the day…my dad, he just lets me have a little bit of space, and lets me do my own thing…because of their personalities. (female, 13 years)

It's their personalities, I think, because dad was the popular one…mum was the more intellectual one…she'd have different ways of finding things out…dad would just ask me straight out, and mum would go round all her spies, she'd be on the phone for like an hour. (female, 14 years)

As these quotes make clear, young people and parents recognised that monitoring and supervision arrangements were fluid, and influenced by the personalities of all those involved.

Conclusions

As demonstrated earlier in this chapter, 'monitoring' and 'supervision' are key terms, frequently used within policy-making circles. The present government, in particular, has stated that it wants to improve monitoring and supervision of children and young people by parents. A wide range of methods and interventions are now available to support this, including group-based parenting programmes, a range of materials and Parenting Orders.

Underlying these policies is a belief that all parents can monitor their children both 'more' and 'more effectively'. This research has suggested that the situation may be more complex than this. Most of the parents in the study were more than aware of their parental responsibilities, and worked extremely hard to keep their children safe and out of trouble. However, we still found that amongst these families there were things that parents did not know, and areas of young people's lives that they had no control over. As many of the parents in the study said, however hard they try, they cannot monitor and supervise children all the time. This has clear implications for policies that are based on parents being legally responsible for their children's behaviour (see Chapter 1 for further discussion of this point). Also, it demonstrates how difficult it may be for many parents to start to monitor and supervise their children 'more', when these processes are embedded so deeply in family relationships and communication.

There are a number of ways in which the findings from this research can be used within the field of family support. First, on *group-based parenting programmes*, the research can be used to demonstrate the strategies that many parents use to monitor and supervise their children. Parents and young people believed that some of these worked well, and some did not work so well. Also, there are some useful examples of where parents felt they could compromise and negotiate, and where they felt they had to 'lay down the law'. How these decisions were explained and discussed with young people are also included in the research. It is also clear that many parents find hearing from *other* parents a particularly valuable learning experience. The research findings could help other parents' voices and ideas to be heard. Of particular importance, we feel, is that *young people's* views can be heard through the research, and can help parents to understand young people's perspectives on these issues.

Second, for those *lobbying and campaigning on behalf of parents and families*, this research provides valuable supporting evidence. Thus, the research shows the considerable effort that this group (and probably most parents) put into protecting and monitoring their children. It also highlights the particular challenges that some groups or families face – for example, mothers with high levels of responsibility for monitoring, or for families living in dangerous localities. The research therefore contributes to the growing evidence base on the realities of parenting today.

Third, in *individual support work* with parents, the results of the research could be used to support parents who are experiencing difficulties. Many parents who are receiving state intervention or support feel guilty, isolated and desperate. The experiences of the parents in this research could be used to reassure parents, demonstrating that all parents – at times – find it difficult to monitor and supervise their child's whereabouts and activities. Whilst few parents in the research had experienced severe difficulties in their parenting, they all faced dilemmas about how best to care for and support their children.

Fourth, *practitioners working to support parents of younger children* may find this research useful to their work. One of the implications of this study is that there are no 'quick fixes' in the teenage years. Rather, monitoring and supervision is embedded in a broader network of relationships and communication styles that are developed throughout a child's lifetime. Thus, practitioners working with parents of younger children could use the research to demonstrate this, focusing on the importance of striving for open and honest communication early on in children's lives.

Finally, the results can be used *to produce materials*, such as leaflets, fliers and group-based activities for parents and young people. A variety of such materials for parents is now produced, to provide information, offer reassurance and give practical hints and tips. The views of the parents and young people in this study could help to bring these topics 'alive', and make them feel real for families. Compared to materials about parenting babies and the under-fives, there is a lack of support material in relation to parenting young people. It should also be mentioned that the authors have already produced materials – a 'Toolkit' of information (Stace and Roker 2006), groupwork activities and resources is now available based on this research.

Learning for practitioners

- 'Monitoring' and 'supervision' are widely used terms, particularly in policy circles, but it is often unclear what people mean by them. Exploring these basic concepts with parents (and other practitioners) is a very useful process.

- Young people in this study were generally accepting of the need for parents to know where they are and what they are doing. However, they were more likely to respond positively to this if (a) decisions and rules were explained to them and (b) some aspects were open to negotiation and compromise.

- Most parents considered that monitoring and supervision was not something that parents could suddenly start doing, or do 'more' of. Rather it was embedded in broader family relationships. Parents therefore considered that monitoring and supervision could not suddenly be 'imposed', but had to build on open communication and trust. The real-life quotes in relation to this could help prompt discussion and debate about these issues.

- The research clearly demonstrates the complexity of monitoring and supervision in families, and the real dilemmas and uncertainties that exist for parents in this respect. The results could be used in supporting funding applications and further work, to support parents in their key task of keeping young people safe.

References

Coleman, J. and Roker, D. (eds) (2001) *Supporting Parents of Teenagers: A Handbook for Professionals.* London: Jessica Kingsley Publishers.

Gillies, V., Ribbens McCarthy, R. and Holland, J. (2001) *Pulling Together, Pulling Apart: The Family Lives of Young People.* York: Joseph Rowntree Foundation.

Stace, S. and Roker, D. (2006) *'Keeping Them Safe' Toolkit.* Brighton: Trust for the Study of Adolescence.

3 'Team parenting' of young people in foster care

Stephanie Stace and Kevin Lowe

In September 1998, the Quality Protects Programme was launched as a five-year programme to improve children's services. The programme outlined national objectives for services for children, young people and families, aiming to ensure that the most vulnerable children in society get the best care, safety and security through well-managed and effective children's services. Local authorities, councillors and social services as 'corporate parents' were expected to think of the standards of care they are providing young people, especially those in care. The programme wanted 'corporate parents', and in particular councillors, to question their decision making in relation to vulnerable young people by asking themselves, 'what if this was my child? Would it be good enough for them? Would it be good enough for me?':

> Think child. More than that – think 'my child'. Would you be happy if a child of your own was moved to a new area and a new home, leaving friends and their familiar school behind? Are you happy that a child for whom you have corporate responsibility is to be moved in this way? ...ask tough questions, and try to find out what the children themselves feel about it. (Armstrong 1999, p.11)

Also, in 2003, the government's Green Paper *Every Child Matters* (DfES 2003) emphasised the importance of a family upbringing for all young people, including those in care. The government's first objective for children's social services is to ensure that all children are securely attached to carers capable of providing safe and effective care for the duration of their childhood. In practice this means secure attachments for young people to carers who are committed to them long term, who support their development, and who guide their transition through childhood to adulthood.

Teenagers in foster care are, in effect, 'parented' by several parties – by the local authority as the 'corporate parent', but in a day-to-day way by others, such as the foster carers they live with and other professionals such as social workers. Some young people's own parents may be closely involved too.

In this chapter, we will not be exploring specifically the role of 'corporate parenting' but instead the notion of 'team parenting'. This refers to a group of people committed to the care of young people in foster care. The team works to ensure that young people in foster care are safe, healthy and have the same opportunities as other young people who are not in care, especially in terms of their education and life opportunities. In this chapter, we will look at who is part of this team, examine the roles they have in caring for young people in foster care, and explore their perceptions of who is actually responsible for young people in foster care.

Background to the study

The Trust for the Study of Adolescence (TSA) carried out a study exploring how parents in 'ordinary' families monitor and supervise young people aged 11 to 16 years (see Chapter 2). The study found that the quality of the parent–child relationship and parent–child communication were core to effective parental monitoring and supervision. Also, the research found that parents were not alone in monitoring and supervising their children, with wider support networks such as family, friends, activity groups and schools also playing a significant part. In most instances, parents relied on other adults in varying situations to monitor their child, keep them safe and ensure their well-being. Parental monitoring and supervision, therefore, was found not to be an isolated activity.

To explore this area further, TSA carried out another research project exploring how *foster carers* monitor, supervise and care for young people aged 13 to 16 years, and also who else is involved in this. It explored the development of relationships between teenagers and their foster carers and other supporting professionals such as social workers (professional support for young people in foster care) and supervising social workers (professional support for foster carers). It also explored how foster carers, social workers and supervising social workers, and any wider support networks, work together as a 'team' to parent young people in foster care.

It is important to note that throughout the research only a few birth parents were interviewed. This was because of a difficulty in recruitment. Therefore, throughout this chapter the issues for birth parents are not specifically addressed. However, the authors do not exclude birth parents from the concept of team parenting of young people in foster care.

About the study

The study was carried out in the UK with the help of one local authority in each country. The local authorities were located in different regional areas, covering inner-city and rural areas. Other organisations such as independent fostering agencies and support groups, who work with foster carers or teenagers in foster care, were also involved. The research was carried out through three different stages:

- *Stage 1*: Focus groups were carried out with teenagers aged 13 to 16 years old in foster care; foster carers of teenagers aged 13 to 16 years old; and social workers and supervising social workers with other supporting professionals. The focus groups discussed issues around how monitoring and supervision are carried out within foster care.

- *Stage 2*: Individual semi-structured interviews were conducted with 40 teenagers, and also with one or both of their foster carers (a total of 56 foster carers were interviewed). Teenagers were selected through variables including: gender; ethnic group; foster family structure; reason for entering foster care; length of time in foster care; contact with birth family; and current issues and behaviours. Twenty-eight social workers supervising social workers and foster care team managers were also interviewed. The individual interviews explored how the interviewees experienced day-to-day monitoring and supervision, and their experiences within foster care.

- *Stage 3*: Each of the young people and their foster carer/s who were individually interviewed in stage 2 were also asked to self-complete a personal record of their whereabouts and activities (teenager) and the young person's whereabouts and activities (foster carer) over a seven-day period.

The foster carers recruited through the local authorities and other organisations ranged from short-term carers to long-term carers. At the time of the interviews, over half of the young people had been in their foster placement for over two years, with a small number of these being in their placement for more than five years. A quarter of the young people had been in their placement for between six months and two years. Only a few young people had been in their placement on a short-term basis of less than six months. The number of long-term foster placements therefore had a significant effect on the research findings around the views of young people, foster carers and supporting professionals who act as 'parents' in foster care.

In this chapter we will focus on one element of the research, which explored who is part of the team that act as the 'parents' of young people in foster care. We explore: the role of the local authorities and professionals such as social workers, foster carers and their supervising social workers; the wider support network of foster carers; and the involvement of young people in their own care. We also explore the perceptions of the participants around who is actually responsible for young people in foster care. Finally, the chapter concludes with what practitioners can learn from this research.

The role of local authorities

What differentiates foster families from 'ordinary' families is that the decision-making process extends beyond the private world of the home and into the public world of the local authority and the courts. A major challenge for social workers, and the care system as a whole, is how to provide care in a way that feels 'ordinary' to young people. Also, parental responsibility within foster care varies depending on the legal status of the child. For example, in some situations the birth parent of the young person in foster care may retain parental responsibility, though in others this may be in the hands of the local authority. In most instances, foster carers do not hold parental responsibility, and are supported by supervising social workers from their local authority, with the young person supported by their social worker. In most cases, young people are the responsibility of the local authority who act as their 'corporate parents'.

Social workers: supporting young people in foster care

Social workers, as representatives of local authorities, provide young people in foster care with support through one-to-one work, working with other professional bodies such as schools, and by ensuring the well-being of the young person whilst living with foster carers. Successful and positive support from social workers to young people in foster care has significant effects, such as reducing the likelihood of foster placement breakdown. Also, the number of social workers a young person has during their time in foster care can affect the development of relationships and the level of consistent support they receive. One study found that only 11 per cent of the young people had one social worker, though 42 per cent had had three or more social workers during their time in foster care (Baldry and Kemmis 1998). This affects the level to which local authorities are successfully acting as corporate parents.

In this study, we asked young people about the support they received from their social workers. A few young people did not hold any particular opinion of their social worker nor did they have any kind of relationship with them. However, about a quarter of the young people said they liked their social worker, appreciated the support they received, felt able to talk to them about problems and worries, and had fun with them. They also appreciated help in life areas, such as developing a hobby or contact with their birth family. For example:

> He [social worker] is a very good friend, I talk to him…it's good because when he comes down I got something to tell him… Like I told him ages ago that I get to go to music club because I like rap…he sorted out when I went to music class and I made a song and CDs. (young male, 16 years)

The majority of young people said they experienced difficulties with their social workers, due to issues such as: frequent changes in who was their social worker; lack of regular visits and contact; social workers being unreliable and untrustworthy; being unable to confide in them; and not liking their social worker's personality. For example:

> I used to get attached to them and whenever they left I cried. And I was young then as well…I was changing homes as well, I had to change my social worker…I didn't like it at all. But now, if they leave – they leave. 'Cos I know how it is, but it happened so much, as you count on your fingers you realise…I haven't seen her [social worker] for so long, and whenever I call her office, her mailbox is full…she says she's gonna come and see me – she doesn't come…I want a new one. (young female, 13 years)

These findings reflect those found in other studies, highlighting the mixed feelings and opinions of young people about their social workers (Baldry and Kemmis 1998; Fletcher 1993; Sinclair, Wilson and Gibbs 2001).

Young people's experiences and opinions of their social workers reflect the sometimes inadequate and unreliable support provided by social workers and local authorities as 'corporate parents'. This may be an area where local authorities and social workers who do not develop successful relationships with young people in their care have to ask themselves: what if this was my child? Would it be good enough for them? Would it be good enough for me?

In this study, we also asked social workers how they felt they supported young people in foster care. Most of the social workers thought that it was important to develop relationships with young people through a number of ways, such as: maintaining regular contact; providing placement and personal support; understanding the young person's interests and developing common ground; enjoying activities and having fun together; developing open lines of communication; and being accessible and reliable. For example:

> It can be a very long and drawn-out process. I think it is just spending time with them, communicating with them, building up a relationship, trying to develop some sort of common ground with them…doing stuff that is mutually enjoyable…and it is with time that we build these relationships. (social worker of young female, 13 years)

However, it was evident from the experiences of the young people in this study that not all of the social workers were providing them with a sufficient level of support. For example, young people often complained about the high turnover of social workers, which prevented long-term relationships being developed. Also, some young people felt they had nothing in common with their social workers, and therefore could not find common ground. Some social workers also recognised this point, with one social worker commenting:

> It would be very naïve to expect that just because you are a social worker that you are going to get on well with this child and they are going to talk to you. At the end of the day they are as human as we are and they will choose who they are going to form relationships with. (social worker of young female, 13 years)

Therefore, though not all young people had negative experiences of the support they receive from their social workers, this was a common experience for many of the young people in this study. This raises the question, are local authorities providing adequate support as corporate parents to young people in foster care?

Foster carers supported by supervising social workers

Foster carers are employed and supported by their local authority to provide day-to-day care for young people in foster care. In this study, we found that foster carers provide day-to-day care for young people in a number of life areas, such as education, health, relationships, maintaining birth family contact and developing life skills towards adulthood. For example, in relation to education, foster carers monitored the young person in their care by keeping in regular contact with their school, keeping track of their progress and achievements, attending parent evenings and educational review meetings and ensuring that the young person completed homework on time. Some foster carers also talked to the young person about their future careers, helping them to plan ahead. As one foster carer said:

> With him being a looked-after child there's a bit more because they have PEP plans, which is a Personal Education Plan. And we get together with the teachers and the caseworker, my case-worker from [local authority] and also the social worker from the borough. We all have a meeting every six months just to check what was going on, if he had any issues, any areas, you

> know, what's going on with his education. But I'm there for
> parent evening when they come up and if there's any meetings
> at the school...I'll go to them. They have a planner with their
> homework which I check every night...we're in contact with
> the school all the time because [young person] didn't settle at all
> well in the beginning... They're [school] ever so good and
> we're in contact regularly. (female foster carer of young male,
> 14 years)

Many foster carers saw themselves in the role of 'parent', including the young person in their care as part of their family network. In providing care for young people, we wanted to find out how foster carers were supported in this role by their supervising social workers, and the level of involvement of supervising social workers in the care of young people in foster care. For most of the foster carers, the support they received was positive and of a high standard, enabling them to ask their supervising social worker for help when it was needed. They appreciated it when supervising social workers were open and honest; good listeners and responsive; accessible and efficient; non-judgemental and reassuring; offered advice and provided resources; shared common interests; and visited regularly. A few foster carers had experienced some problems with their supervising social workers, and these centred mainly around inadequate cover during maternity leave; being untrustworthy; and being unemotional and 'following the book' too much.

Most of the foster carers noticed a significant difference between the positive support they received from their supervising social workers, and the lack of support young people sometimes received from their social workers. For example:

> We see him [supervising social worker] every six weeks and
> that's regular. He's on the end of the telephone so now I can
> always chat and he comes around and takes the children out. So,
> we have a good relationship. Social workers, it's really difficult
> because they seem to change so often...[social worker] went off
> on maternity leave for the summer holidays and we never had
> any contact from the beginning of the summer holidays...as far
> as another social worker we haven't heard anything. (female
> foster carer of young male, 14 years)

Therefore, these findings support those of other studies such as Padbury and Frost (2002), where a lack of support from social workers was considered to have a negative effect on problem solving, compared to supervising social workers (link workers) who were found to be the 'backbone' of support for foster carers.

In this study we also interviewed supervising social workers and discussed how they felt they supported foster carers in caring for young people. They commented that in order to build quality relationships with foster carers it was important that they: were open, honest and reliable; were there in times of need; maintained regular face-to-face contact, especially for new carers; introduced them to training and other foster carers; and were respectful and true to their word. Supervising social workers felt that relationships with foster carers often took a long time to develop, and that it was important from the outset that roles were established and foster carers knew what the supervising social worker role involved. They were aware that during difficult times, their role must remain objective, and always keep the interests of the young person paramount. Therefore, through supporting foster carers, supervising social workers were found to have a direct and significant role in 'parenting' young people in foster care.

Foster carers' support networks

Studies have found that foster carers regularly receive help in caring for young people from different formal and informal sources (Farmer, Moyers and Lipscombe 2004). Formal sources include family placement workers, social workers, schools, general practitioners (GPs) and other foster carers. Informal sources include the foster carer's partner, children, parents, other relatives, friends, neighbours and the wider community.

In this study, we found that the majority of foster carers relied on a variety of formal and informal support networks when they needed support or advice. Formal support included social workers and supervising social workers, schools and other foster carers. These findings reflect those of Farmer *et al.* (2004) who also found family placement workers (supervising social workers), the young person's social worker, schools, GPs and other foster carers as the most readily available useful support.

However, this study found that, to help with the practicalities of day-to-day life, foster carers relied more on informal support networks such as family (parents, birth children and siblings), friends, neighbours, activity leaders, the church and other foster carers. These support networks helped the foster carers with babysitting needs, respite care, supporting the young person's needs and general day-to-day domestic activities. For example:

> My mum's quite involved, and she lives just down the road...and my sisters when they're around...they are involved as the wider family. She [young person] would see them as her family...her youth leaders at church would monitor her. I think school have been fantastic, and they've always kept a close eye on [young person]...and our friends are great, I couldn't do it without my friends. (female foster carer of young female, 14 years)

Farmer *et al.* (2004) also found that the most readily available and useful informal support to foster carers were their partner, their birth children, their parents, other relatives, friends, and neighbours.

The foster carers in this study valued the support networks they had, and recognised how involved the wider family and community were in supporting them as foster carers. The involvement of support networks in helping foster carers to provide a safe and positive environment for young people in their care and to develop and grow into adulthood, is important when reflecting on who is part of 'team parenting', from the local authority to the local community.

Involvement of young people in their own care

The Children Act (1989) states that local authorities are required to take into account the wishes and feelings of children in their care (Thomas and O'Kane 1998). Also, Article 12 of the United Nations Convention on the Rights of the Child states that young people in foster care should be involved in the decision-making processes concerning the judicial and administrative proceedings and the care they receive. Also, the government's Quality Protects initiative that was launched in 1998, asked local authorities to 'listen to children and young people, in planning services and in monitoring outcomes' and stated that 'consulting with children and young people can become as central and routine as any other democratic process' (Armstrong 1999, p.12).

It is important for young people in foster care to be able to voice their opinions, to feel heard and to influence their own lives. Young people need to be aware of their own care plan, and feel able to speak openly in their review meetings and to supporting adults. This empowers young people, reduces the risk of placement breakdown and enables them to find solutions to their problems (Baldry and Kemmis 1998; Lipscombe, Farmer and Moyers 2003). However, young people in foster care may feel vulnerable and unable to make complaints due to consequences this could have on their relationships with their carers or supporting social worker (Gilligan 2000). Also, the quality of the relationships between teenagers, foster carers and social workers are central to enabling young people to disclose their feelings about the care they are receiving. The core triangle of dialogue, between the young person, foster carer and social worker has been found to be the most significant to young people (Padbury and Frost 2002).

To explore how young people openly disclosed their feelings about the care they receive in their day-to-day lives, we asked them who they confided in and talked to when they were worried about something or had any problems. We found that many of the young people felt they could talk to their foster carers, especially those with positive relationships. However, some young people said that they did not talk to anyone, and only relied on themselves, feeling able to sort out any problems or difficulties they may go through. Only a few young people felt they were able to talk to their social workers, with many stating that they did not see them enough to build the kind of relationship that would enable them to talk openly about their feelings. Therefore, it was evident that young people in foster care talked mostly to their foster carers if they were worried or had any problems.

Foster carers and supporting professionals were also asked who they thought young people confided in when they needed to talk to someone. Both foster carers and social workers and supervising social workers felt that young people should be able to talk to their foster carers first and foremost if they had any worries or concerns. Foster carers were seen by themselves and social workers and supervising social workers as '24-hour care', and therefore in contact with the child on a daily basis. Therefore, it was seen as the responsibility of the foster carer to help the young person through any day-to-day issues.

To explore the involvement of young people in their own care further, we also asked the young people about their involvement in and their experiences of review meetings, and whether they felt they were of any benefit to them. Most of the young people attended their review meetings, though many out of routine rather than commitment. A quarter of the young people interviewed felt that review meetings were beneficial to them, as they enabled them to voice their opinions about their own care, and enabled them to talk about problems. The young people also felt that review meetings enabled issues to be resolved, which resulted in more positive outcomes for them. For example:

> They're good because you can have your say and then it'll get passed on and you get listened to and stuff. (young male, 15 years)

However, another quarter of the young people felt that although they attended their review meetings, they saw them as a repetitive process, and not one through which anything significant was achieved. Therefore, these young people paid little attention to what was being discussed in review meetings even though they attended them.

Approximately half of the young people had negative experiences of their review meetings. They did not feel that reviews resolved any issues, and often felt in an uncomfortable position or excluded from discussions. These young people described feelings associated with being disempowered and having no influence on the care they received, including:

- being unable to speak honestly about care due to the presence of a foster carer
- feeling intimidated when asked questions by the review panel
- birth parents' and/or foster carer's negative reactions to their views
- being talked 'about' but not included in discussions or asked for opinions
- plans agreed in meetings not being realised.

For example:

> I still don't like to have to talk in big groups because I know if I
> say something in front of my mum and dad they'll go mad if it's
> something I've said wrong sort of thing, because they kind of
> go over the top a little bit if you do something wrong...when
> they sit about talking to you and then they, like, ask you a
> question and you sit there quiet and they say well, why aren't
> you answering the questions, it's like well I have no comment on
> that really. It's like saying I want to say something but I can't.
> (young male, 16 years)

Therefore, though most of the young people attended their review meetings, only a quarter of the young people found them to be beneficial, with the majority finding them either repetitive and useless, or something that can cause them distress and discomfort. These findings reflect those of other studies in which young people found their review meetings boring, irrelevant, frustrating and disempowering (Hogan and Sinclair 1997). This raises the question of how much young people are actually involved in the planning of their own care. Similar to the findings of this study, Padbury and Frost (2002) argued that 'statutory childcare reviews offer a valuable framework for collating young people's views, but it would appear local authorities are missing these opportunities' (p.79).

Who is responsible for teenagers in foster care?

From the findings so far, it is evident that there are a number of key individuals who have a significant role in caring for young people in foster care. The role of the 'corporate parent' and the notion of 'team parenting' led us to ask young people, foster carers, social workers and supervising social workers, who they perceived to be responsible for young people in foster care, and to what degree. Who is responsible for ensuring the young person's needs and life opportunities are being met?

We found that approximately a third of young people said that they are responsible for themselves, and their well-being and future plans. They were aware of the support they received from foster carers and social workers (in some instances) though they saw the primary responsibility as their own. However, in contrast, the majority of young people saw their foster carers as responsible for them, as it was their job, they were living as part of their family and 'under their roof', or they were acting as their 'parent'. For example:

> Well because I'm living under their roof and it's up to them to look after me and stuff. I mean it's also up to me. (young female, 14 years)

> I think it's her [foster carer] responsibility… Because she is the guardian isn't she, she is and it is her job like that is what she wanted to do…with a child like me she would have to be concerned and [I] ask her things and you know, just talk to her about all different things because I think that with a child like me it makes me feel more wanted and more respected in the end. (young female, 15 years)

In comparison, none of the foster carers stated that the young people were responsible for themselves. Most of the foster carers regarded themselves as responsible for the young person in their care. Many foster carers used the terms 'treat them like my own children', 'that's my job', 'as a parent', or as being a 'stand-in parent'. For example:

> I'm his foster mum and it's everyday issues…so it's my responsibility. Obviously if I need any advice or anything I've got backup case workers to talk to if I needed anything but at the end of the day they're mine. (female foster carer of young male, 14 years)

The opinions of the social workers and supervising social workers were in contrast to those of foster carers and young people. The majority saw social workers as primarily responsible for the young person and their welfare. Social workers and supervising social workers saw caring for a young person in foster care as a joint responsibility between foster carers, social workers and supervising social workers, with inputs from organisations such as schools and support services. Foster carers were seen by most social workers and supervising social workers as the day-to-day carers, supported and guided by them. However, foster carers were only regarded as *primarily* responsible for young people in their care by a few social workers. For example:

I think we all have a responsibility. I think unfortunately as social workers we feel like it all lies on our shoulders because we carry a care order which gives us a share of that responsibility and therefore if there is a parent who is not in the primary role of looking after a child and something goes wrong for that child then it falls to the [local authority] to know why that is. But the reality of our day-to-day practicalities is that we can't maybe oversee all of those issues on a daily basis, so we do empower a lot of that responsibility to the person that is in primary care…that would mostly be the residential worker, the relative carer, the foster carer or the family member. (social worker of young male, 16 years)

Responsibility therefore was seen to primarily rest in the hands of the local authority and the young person's social worker. However, there was no consensus amongst social workers, supervising social workers, foster carers and young people about who was actually responsible for parenting young people in foster care. Therefore, it is questionable whether the roles of those who are responsible for young people in foster care are clearly defined, and whether this is an area that needs more discussion.

Learning for practitioners

- The concept of parenting within foster care needs to be clearly defined for the key parties involved in looking after the young person. It appears to be taken for granted, rather than explored explicitly, especially when young people are with long-term carers. This will enable young people to understand who has parental responsibility for them in different areas during their time in foster care.

- The role of supporting networks, and in particular the role of foster carers' wider families and friends, needs to be recognised. Foster carers 'parent' young people with much support from their families and friends, and rarely in isolation.

- The number of short-term relationships between young people and their social workers continues to be a serious concern. The high turnover of social workers seriously undermines the notion of consistent parenting.

- 'Team parenting' could be explored more explicitly to enable foster carers, social workers, supervising social workers, young people and wider support networks to work together.

References

Armstrong, H. (1999) *Think Child! The Councillor's Guide to Quality Protects.* London: Department of Health.

Baldry, S. and Kemmis, J. (1998) 'What is it like to be looked after by a local authority?' *British Journal of Social Work 28*, 1, 129–136.

DfES (Department for Education and Skills) (2003) *Every Child Matters.* London: The Stationery Office.

Farmer, E., Moyers, S. and Lipscombe, J. (2004) *Fostering Adolescents.* London: Jessica Kingsley Publishers.

Fletcher, B. (1993) *Not Just a Name: The Views of Young People in Foster and Residential Care.* London: The National Consumer Council.

Gilligan, R. (2000) 'The importance of listening to the child in foster care.' In G. Kelly and R. Gilligan (eds) *Issues in Foster Care: Policy, Practice & Research.* London: Jessica Kingsley Publishers.

Hogan, G. and Sinclair, R. (1997) 'Children and young people's participation in review.' In G. Hogan and R. Sinclair (eds) *Planning for Children in Care in Northern Ireland.* London: National Children's Bureau.

Lipscombe, J., Farmer, E. and Moyers, S. (2003) 'Parenting fostered adolescents: skills and strategies.' *Child and Family Social Work 8*, 4, 243–255.

Padbury, P. and Frost, N. (2002) 'Solving problems in foster care: key issues for young people, foster carers and social services.' *Child and Family Social Work 8*, 3, 238–239.

Sinclair, I., Wilson, K. and Gibbs, I. (2001) 'A life more ordinary': what children want from foster placements.' *Adoption & Fostering 25*, 4, 17–26.

The Children Act (1989) London: The Stationery Office.

Thomas, N. and O'Kane, C. (1998) 'When children's wishes and feelings clash with their "best interests".' *The International Journal of Children's Rights 6*, 2, 137–154.

4 Family communication about alcohol

Louise Cox, Nigel Sherriff, Lester Coleman and Debi Roker

This chapter describes research into a key aspect of family life – how parents of young people communicate about, and attempt to supervise, their children's alcohol use. This is a key issue given the recent evidence of an increase in alcohol use amongst young people, particularly in relation to binge and chronic drinking. The chapter provides a brief background to the topic, describes the research and summarises the main findings and their implications.

Introduction

In recent years, concerns over alcohol misuse have become central to government policy. This is due to two issues – alcohol-related crime and antisocial behaviour, and risks to young people's health as a result of binge drinking. In 2004, the Prime Minister's Strategy Unit published the *Alcohol Harm Reduction Strategy for England* (Cabinet Office 2004), which outlined plans for tackling the problems associated with alcohol misuse. The strategy explicitly acknowledged the importance of families in 'making the strategy happen' (p.19), by parents providing young people with 'clear and accurate information, and encouragement to make responsible decisions' (p.20).

It is well known that parents can affect the development of their children's drinking behaviour. For example, Barnes and her colleagues (2000) showed how parenting styles can predict adolescents' initial drinking levels, as well as their rates of future alcohol use. The authors conclude that effective parenting is an important factor in preventing alcohol misuse. Indeed, there is an increasing awareness of the role that parents can have in reducing the incidence and impact of alcohol misuse upon young people (Barnes *et al.* 2000; Orford and Velleman 2002; Spoth, Redmond and Shin 2001). A number of studies have demonstrated how some adolescents imitate the alcohol consumption of their parents, and in particular, their fathers (for example, Yu 2003; Zhang, Welte and Wieczorek 1999). Yu (2003) demonstrated that parents' control of underage alcohol use in the household can successfully reduce children's involvement with alcohol.

There is clear evidence that sensible parental drinking, combined with open communication and moderate levels of parental supervision, is most likely to lead to a reduction in alcohol-related harm (Beinart *et al.* 2002; Foxcroft and Lowe 1991, 1995; Newburn and Shiner 2001). For instance, Highet (2005) found that communicating and negotiating openly with children seems to be an effective strategy in helping young people develop and sustain a sensible relationship with alcohol. Highet found that recreational drinking, including by young people who are under age, is often a normal part of family life. She reports that many parents engage in discussion and negotiation with their children as a way of initiating them into safe and socially responsible drinking. In contrast, harsh and controlling approaches, or resigned tolerance, appeared to be less effective. However, despite these advances in understanding, little attention has been given to describing *how* parent/young person communication and supervision in relation to alcohol actually takes place (Ennett *et al.* 2001). This was the aim of the study described in this chapter.

Two studies recently undertaken at the Trust for the Study of Adolescence (TSA) have provided some insights into family processes and alcohol, although this was not the main aim of either study. First, Stace and Roker (2005) in a study of *parental monitoring and supervision* found that many parents find it hard to supervise alcohol consumption. They found that parental supervision was based mainly on intuition, and varied considerably in effectiveness. Second, research into young people's *underage risky drinking* (Coleman and Cater 2005) found that many young people would welcome information and skills around alcohol to be communicated by their parents. For the few who had received more open communication, there was some evidence of a reduction in alcohol-related harm. Both studies showed that many parents lack guidance in conveying sensible drinking messages to young people. The research described in this chapter aimed to explore this further.

The research

There were two main aims of the research. One aim was to explore parents' views about young people and alcohol use, and any concerns or issues they might have about it. We wanted to explore the strategies that parents use to communicate about alcohol, and whether (and if so how) they try to supervise young people's drinking. An additional aim was to explore what information and support parents wanted in this respect.

The first stage of the project involved having another look at the two TSA studies mentioned earlier. Five main themes emerged in relation to how parents and young people 'relate' about alcohol. These were:

- *communication* – examples of parents discussing alcohol with young people

- *supervision* – examples of parents trying to monitor, supervise or control young people's use of alcohol

- *modelling* – instances of parents mentioning their own use of alcohol, or how their alcohol use might be seen by their children

- *legal and health issues* – information about what parents know about the law in relation to young people and alcohol, or about health issues (for example, alcohol units)

- *difficult issues* – examples of how parents address 'difficult' issues that arise in relation to alcohol (for example, a young person wanting alcohol to take to a party, or coming home drunk).

We then conducted some new research with 40 parents to explore these areas further. All the parents had young people aged 13–17 and were recruited via a number of means, including newsletters, advertising, local universities and the local council. The sample included mothers and fathers, a range of family structures and circumstances, and parents from different social backgrounds. Each person was interviewed individually, usually in their own homes. The information was then analysed according to the five themes above. The main results are given below.

Main findings

The main results from the study are given under the following six headings:

- young people and alcohol use: what are parents concerned about?

- communication

- supervision

- modelling and influences

- legal and health issues

- difficult issues.

Young people and alcohol use: what are parents concerned about?

Parents talked about a wide range of issues associated with young people and alcohol use. These related to three main areas: health implications, practical concerns and worries about the 'drinking culture'.

First, many parents raised concerns over the health implications of young people drinking alcohol. These were concerns about short-term effects, such as being sick, falling over, fighting etc., as well as longer-term implications, such as alcoholism. For example:

> ...the health issue is a real problem for me, 'cos once you've had so much to drink, you, you've no idea what's going on. (mother of one, 13 years)

> The thing I worry about is that if they carry on doing it at such a young age, and then they start drinking more, and I think quite a lot of 'em by the time they're in their mid-20s or 30s, they're gonna end up alcoholics, and there's the health issues, as well. (mother of one, 15 years)

Second, parents talked about their concerns in relation to the practical and risk issues associated with young people and alcohol. For example, they talked about where young people drink alcohol, the type of alcohol that young people consume (with particular concerns about alco-pops), the availability of alcohol to young people, and the amount of alcohol consumed by young people at one time e.g. binge drinking. For example:

> Because obviously, you get a lot of like, the alco-pops drinks – which are very – you know – fruit juice which have got alcohol in, and you wouldn't necessarily realise that it's alcohol. I think kids just drink it as if it's juice. (mother of one, 13 years)

> It's the volume to which they drink, in the circumstance. You know, if you're drinking slowly all day, it's very different to drinking a large amount on an empty stomach – because that's what children do. There's so much available now and children look that much older. The shopkeepers have a challenge on their hands as well, to determine that someone's the age that they are. (mother of two, 13 years and 16 years)

Finally in this section, parents talked about young people's attitudes towards drinking and alcohol use, with several parents making references to the 'drinking culture' and the impact of the mass media. This was highlighted in particular by those parents from black and minority ethnic groups, who differentiated between the way that alcohol is often used in the UK and the way that it is used in other cultures:

> I think for me, I mean, I do have a problem with the attitude that I feel is part of our culture, really that it's great to go out and get absolutely – like my son would say – rat-arsed. (mother of one, 13 years)

> I think for me, growing up in the Chinese culture, alcohol was not something that's in common use with young people. Not in the way that it's used in this country. (mother of one, 15 years)

The following section picks up on some of these issues, discussing how parents and young people communicate about alcohol.

Communication

Four main themes arose in relation to communication about alcohol. These were: general communication issues, messages that parents try and portray, difficult issues in relation to communication and 'successful' approaches.

In terms of specific techniques or strategies for talking about alcohol within the family, one of the main ways of initiating conversation was to use examples of personal, family or peer experiences. For example, many parents reported basing a conversation around their own encounters with alcohol. Other 'conversation starters' included using a specific incident when a friend or family member was drunk or ill as a result of excessive alcohol use, and using this as a timely basis for discussion within the family. For example:

> We have talked about it when one of the older one's friends drank way too much once…so we were able to talk about it after that. (mother of one, 14 years)

Parents talked about a wide range of messages that they try to portray to young people in relation to alcohol use. One of the main messages was that of 'moderation', and that when used in a safe and sensible way, alcohol can be a normal part of adult life. Other messages parents felt were important to give to young people related to personal safety, the law regarding young people and alcohol, and the health implications of misusing alcohol. Less common, but very important to some parents, were messages concerned with the amounts of alcohol young people drink, the type of alcohol and the fact that alcohol can become addictive. For example:

> What I'm trying to say is I think that, for most people, drinking alcohol is part of their social lives and therefore it's something that you can enjoy but also carry certain risks with it, as well. (mother of two, 14 years and 15 years)

Parents also talked about a number of difficult issues in relation to communicating with young people about alcohol. First, parents worried that if they explicitly asked young people not to do something, they would be more likely to do the very thing that they have been asked not to do. Second, parents talked about the need to try and reach some sort of communicative 'balance'. For example, many parents said that they did not want to pry or interfere, and wanted to ensure the development of independence and personal choice in their child. For example:

> I think it's the same old thing, if your parents tell you something, unless you are the perfect child, you're either not gonna take any notice of them, or you're gonna go and try whatever it is they've told you not to. (mother of one, 17 years)

Parents were also asked whether anything had helped with communication about alcohol in their family. These included that of talking 'little and often' regarding the consequences and implications of alcohol use, and providing young people with clear messages and information. Further, parents talked about the need to ensure that young people are given the chance to initiate conversations when they are 'in the mood' for talking. Negotiation about rules and boundaries were also considered very important. This negotiation required parents to respect young people and view them as young adults, whilst at the same time ensuring that communication lines are kept open between young people and themselves. In addition, parents said that 'normalising' alcohol use, rather than forbidding it, helped initiate open and general communication. For example:

> ...it was always our intention to talk about alcohol in a way that he doesn't feel he's being talked down to. And allowing him to express interest, concern, ask questions and so on. So, it's always been an open discussion between the two – well, three of us. (father of one, 15 years)

There were other aspects of communicating with young people about alcohol that parents felt were important: the use of humour, language that young people can relate to and the use of personal and family experiences of alcohol/alcoholism to initiate conversation. For example:

> ...if you're going to discuss anything, a conclusion that I came to earlier on, was – is the use of language. And if you restrict the language that they're able to use – as you're inclined to – and by that, I mean things like four-letter words and all the rest of it – if you restrict the use of those, you can't get the full message across. (father of one, 15 years)

The following section outlines how parents described their attempts to monitor and supervise young people's alcohol use.

Supervision

Three main issues arose in relation to parents' supervision of alcohol within the family: rules and limitations, difficult issues in relation to supervision and 'successful' approaches.

When asked about specific limitations or rules in relation to alcohol supervision, few parents had any. For example, some parents said that in most circumstances a parent simply has to trust a young person and that young people cannot be 'managed' or 'controlled'.

> It's difficult to impose any limits, 'cos you're not actually physically there and with teenagers, you have to give them a measure of independence and encourage them to sort of, regulate themselves, to a degree, with parental encouragement and boundary setting. (father of two, 14 years and 17 years)

However, many parents did attempt to limit the *type* of alcohol young people were allowed. Here parents differentiated between 'softer' alcoholic drinks such as beer and lager, versus 'harder' drinks such as spirits. Parents also made reference to alco-pops, with many concerned that young people did not recognise their alcoholic content. For example:

> Well, it's usually – I've always said, you can drink beer, weak beer. Not strong beer and not those horrible alco-pop things. I would never ever have them in my house, or spirits. (mother of one, 15 years)

Parents reported a number of difficult issues that they had encountered in relation to the supervision of young people's alcohol use. Some parents said that they did not want to impose harsh limitations on their children, particularly if it would make young people stand out and appear different to their friends. Other parents reported that one of the main difficult issues to deal with was negotiation. Several parents commented on the dilemma that if a young person is going to drink alcohol anyway, then to what extent should a parent supply alcohol or allow alcohol in the home. These issues were closely related to safety, with some parents saying that they would prefer a young person and his/her friends to drink alcohol in the home, as opposed to drinking outside of the home, which might lead to them approaching strangers and asking them to buy alcohol. For example:

> …I probably aid and abet, because every Friday I buy a tray of cans which they have to pay me half for, 'cos it's cheaper than them getting it from the off licence, so probably in a way, I'm being a bad mother 'cos I'm helping them get it. (mother of one, 17 years)

There was a range of other issues or concerns described by parents. These included: other parents' attitudes towards young people and alcohol, a young person's reaction to limitations or rules that a parent may try to impose, and knowing whether they (parents) should be worried about young people's alcohol use. For example:

> I really don't know if I should be or I shouldn't be [worried] because there are people who are doing lots worse – sort of, taking drugs and drinking a lot more, and given that he's doing well at college and he works hard...I don't know if his drinking is a problem or not. (mother of one, 17 years)

Some parents talked about 'successful' approaches or ways of supervising a young person's use of alcohol. The main successful approach involved using some form of negotiation with young people. Many parents said that negotiating with young people, and letting them experiment with alcohol in a safe and supervised environment, was the most appropriate approach to supervising alcohol use within the family. For example:

> At her age, we negotiate. Well, because she's a young adult and it's part of growing up, isn't it? And being an adult and being seen to be an adult. For me to respect her – for her to able to put her case to me, and me to put mine to her. And for us to find something that, hopefully, works for both us. I just think it's a good life lesson, anyway. (mother of two, 15 years and 17 years)

The following section explores how parents modelled, or felt they influenced, young people's alcohol use.

Modelling and influences

Parents in the research ranged from abstainers to heavier drinkers in terms of their own alcohol use, with the majority drinking at moderate levels. Most of the parents said that their children were fully aware of parental alcohol use, and many parents felt that this had no (or very little) impact upon their children's own use of alcohol.

Where parents talked about their children seeing them drunk or ill as a result of alcohol use, the majority felt that this amused young people and did not have a negative impact on them. When asked to say what young people might learn from witnessing or observing parental use of alcohol, the majority of parents felt that young people were receiving mainly positive messages. These messages were associated with moderation and seeing alcohol as a part of normal social life. For example:

> I think he's learned that it's OK to drink in moderation. And that's the message I hope he gets, 'cos he doesn't see me drinking all the time, usually just social. And so, that's what I hope to get across to him. (mother of one, 15 years)

Interestingly, most parents were more concerned about the influence of factors outside of the home than the influence of their behaviour as parents. The most commonly reported influence on young people's attitudes to alcohol was that of friends and the peer group. Many parents recognised that friends and social groups are key in determining the use of alcohol by young people, and some believed that young people are more likely to listen to their friends than they are to their parents. Additionally, several parents expressed concern about mass-media advertising, which they felt was often aimed specifically at young people, especially in relation to alco-pops.

A final modelling influence that arose as being important for parents in relation to young people and alcohol, was the British 'drinking culture'. Some parents made reference to the new licensing laws (Licensing Act 2003) and again the issue of the type of alcohol that some young people drink. For example, many parents made reference to alco-pops as an issue of particular current concern and importance:

> I think there is a culture now that encourages drinking. You know, the fact, well, and it's not just drinking. It's right across the board – you've got (um) things like this new drinking – opening hours – I think is absolutely stupid. (father of one, 15 years)

The next section explores the legal and health issues that parents talked about.

Legal and health issues

Parents were asked about the legal and health issues in relation to young people and alcohol use. Many parents felt confident that both they and young people were generally aware of the broad legal issues associated with alcohol use – for example the age at which young people are allowed to buy alcohol. However, parents reported being less aware of the specific legalities in relation to young people and alcohol – such as the age at which young people can drink alcohol with a meal on licensed premises. Furthermore, the majority of parents felt they were not aware of alcohol units or 'sensible' drinking guidelines and agreed that their children were also unlikely to be aware of these.

Parents had further concerns about legal and health issues in relation to their children and alcohol. These included emotional vulnerability, safety and the behavioural effects of alcohol (for example, fighting, being out of control and drink spiking). Several parents also made reference at this point to gender differences in relation to young people and alcohol use, and about the potential increase in vulnerability and risk for teenage young women associated with alcohol use:

> ...I think especially having a daughter – I just think it makes her a lot more vulnerable, if she's drinking, I do worry a lot. (father of one, 13 years)

Parents generally wanted more information with regards to the legal and health implications of alcohol use. Some parents said that this information should be in a format that was accessible to young people:

> Yeah, I think it's good for children to know that as well. How many units are in certain things, 'cos they probably wouldn't even realise. Especially like with the alco-pops drinks that are like fruit juice and with alcohol mixed in. You certainly wouldn't know what sort of unit that is and how much that they can have of that. Even though they're not supposed to be drinking it, but yeah, I think that would be useful information. (mother of one, 13 years)

Difficult issues

Parents revealed a number of situations or incidents that they found difficult to deal with in relation to their children and alcohol use. The most common incidents reported included: their child (or someone within their child's peer group) getting very drunk, or getting into trouble with the police as a result of alcohol use. For example:

> My son was in trouble because he'd gone into an off-licence and – 'cos he was tall – bought the drink for a group of friends and got into trouble for it. (female, mother of one, 16 years)

> Well, yeah, there have been some incidents recently – he got drunk outside school and got arrested and spent a night in the cells. (mother of one, 14 years)

Several parents also said that they found the attitudes of other parents difficult to deal with. This was particularly the case when parents of their children's peers had rules and limitations that conflicted with their own:

> …they [the parents] seem to be letting her daughter get away with going out late at night, often not coming back 'til 12 o'clock and drinking heavily, and my daughter still wanting to, to hang around with her, and meet her in the evenings, sometimes. That's been tough. (father of two, 13 years and 17 years)

Other difficult issues parents raised included alcohol going missing in the house and the dilemma that if a young person is going to drink anyway, should a parent supply alcohol and allow alcohol in the house. For example:

> But, you know, he's gonna drink anyway. But then he'll be doing it out in a park somewhere or something, or out on the street. And I've always said to him, you're not drinking in the street. So, now he will say, well can I, can I have a few beers before I go out? (mother of one, 15 years)

These sorts of issues and dilemmas were common in the families involved in the research. Few parents had any set responses or methods for dealing with them, but rather addressed them as and when they arose.

Conclusions

This chapter provides some insights into how parents communicate with their children about alcohol and how they seek to supervise sensible drinking in the family. The research identified a number of related experiences, as well as concerns and worries that parents had.

It is important to stress, of course, that the views of the parents expressed here only represent one 'side' of the equation. The research did not explore young people's views and experiences, and so we do not know whether what parents are saying is accurate. Crucially, we also do not know whether what parents viewed as 'effective' strategies in relation to communication about alcohol, actually had any effect on young people's views, attitudes or behaviours.

Despite this, the research is important in providing new information about how parents view communication about alcohol in the family and the issues that alcohol raises. It is significant that most of the parents interviewed said that they wanted more information about young people and alcohol use. They also wanted advice and support in relation to communicating and negotiating about these issues. The four main things that parents wanted were:

- 'hints and tips' for opening up discussion about alcohol
- suggestions and ideas in relation to monitoring and supervising young people's use of alcohol
- more information in relation to legal and health issues, including accurate information about recommended 'units', and the law in relation to when, where and what young people can drink
- ideas and strategies that other parents have used to deal with difficult issues and situations in relation to alcohol.

These are key and important issues, and there is no reason to believe that this group of parents is in any way unusual in wanting more information and advice in these areas. Interestingly, they reflect the findings from the chapter on websites (Roker, Chapter 9), when a group of parents were asked to find information on the internet about young people and alcohol. Many found this difficult, and it was clear that many parents had inaccurate and out-of-date information in relation to this topic.

It is therefore important that more information and support is provided to parents in order to help them to open up conversations about alcohol. In addition, parents would welcome help and support to monitor and supervise young people in this respect, to help to keep them safe. The authors have addressed this issue in one particular way. We have produced a 12-page 'newsletter' for parents, which includes 'hints and tips', legal information, agony aunt/uncle columns, etc. This newsletter is now being used by parents of young people and by practitioners who work with parents. Further information about this newsletter is available from TSA.

Learning for practitioners

- Most parents find it difficult to open up conversations with young people about alcohol use.

- Parents want more practical 'hints and tips' to help them to open up conversations about a range of difficult issues, including alcohol.

- A number of parents in this study felt they did have useful ideas for successfully opening up conversations about alcohol. These included talking about their own history/experience of alcohol use. Sharing these strategies with other parents would be very useful.

- A number of parents also felt that certain strategies worked well in relation to encouraging sensible drinking among young people. These included letting young people experiment with alcohol at home, and not 'mystifying' alcohol. These strategies could be promoted to other parents as ideas for them to try.

- Most parents wanted simple and clear information about legal and health issues – for example the recommended 'units' for alcohol intakes, and the law in relation to young people and alcohol. Providing this might help some parents to feel more prepared about talking to young people.

- Many parents did not feel they knew what was 'normal' in relation to young people and alcohol. Providing details of specialist organisations that can provide more information about this would be very useful.

- There are a number of good 'real-life' examples in this chapter of difficult issues that parents had faced in relation to young people and alcohol – for example whether to buy alcohol for young people who were under 18 years of age. These could be used by those working with parents to explore different options and scenarios in relation to difficult issues.

References

Barnes, G.M., Refman, A.S., Farrell, M.P. and Dintcheff, B.A. (2000) 'The effects of parenting on the development of adolescent alcohol misuse: a six-wave latent growth model.' *Journal of Marriage and the Family 62*, 1, 175–186.

Beinart, S., Anderson, B., Lee, S. and Utting, D. (2002) *Youth at Risk? A National Survey of Risk Factors, Protective Factors and Problem Behaviour Among Young People in England, Scotland and Wales.* London: Communities that Care.

Cabinet Office (2004) *Alcohol Harm Reduction Strategy for England.* London: Cabinet Office.

Coleman, L. and Cater, S. (2005) *Underage 'Risky' Drinking: Motivations and Outcomes.* York: Joseph Rowntree Foundation.

Ennett, S.T., Bauman, K.E., Foshee, V.A., Pemberton, M. and Hicks, K.A. (2001) 'Parent–child communication about adolescent tobacco and alcohol use: what do parents say and does it affect youth behavior?' *Journal of Marriage and the Family 63*, 1, 48–62.

Foxcroft, D.R. and Lowe, G. (1991) 'Adolescent drinking behaviour and family socialization factors: a meta-analysis.' *Journal of Adolescence 14*, 3, 255–273.

Foxcroft, D.R. and Lowe, G. (1995) 'Adolescent drinking, smoking and other substance use involvement: links with perceived family life.' *Journal of Adolescence 18*, 2, 159–177.

Highet, G. (2005) 'Alcohol and cannabis: young people talking about how parents respond to their use of these two drugs.' *Drugs: Education, Prevention, and Policy, 12*, 2, 113–124.

Newburn, T. and Shiner, M. (2001) *Teenage Kicks? Young People and Alcohol: A Review of the Literature.* York: Joseph Rowntree Foundation.

Orford, J. and Velleman, R. (2002) 'Families and alcohol problems.' In: Alcohol Research Forum (eds) *100% Proof: Research for Action on Alcohol.* London: Alcohol Concern.

Spoth, R.L., Redmond, C. and Shin, C. (2001) 'Randomized trial of brief family interventions for general populations: adolescent substance use outcomes four years following baseline.' *Journal of Consulting and Clinical Psychology 69*, 4, 1–15.

Stace, S. and Roker, D. (2005) *Monitoring and Supervision in 'Ordinary' Families: The Views and Experiences of Young People Aged 11–16 and their Parents/Carers.* York: Joseph Rowntree Foundation.

Yu, J. (2003) 'The association between parental alcohol-related behaviours and children's drinking.' *Drug and Alcohol Dependence 69*, 3, 253–262.

Zhang, L., Welte, J.W. and Wieczorek, W.F. (1999) 'The influence of parental drinking and closeness on adolescent drinking.' *Journal of Studies on Alcohol 60*, 2, 245–251.

5 Children's move to secondary school: what do parents need at this time?

Debi Roker, Kerry Devitt and Amanda Holt

Given the importance of the transition to secondary school for children, and their parents, it is remarkable that there is not more information and research available. Much of the work that has been done has focused on specific aspects, such as academic progression between primary and secondary school (see, for example, Galton, Gray and Ruddock 1999). Much less is known about children's broader experiences at this time.

For many children, the move to secondary school will be one of the major events of their life, signifying a developmental shift from the world of childhood, to adolescence and young adulthood (see, for example, Christensen *et al.* 1999; Tabor 1993). For children, there are many notable changes between primary and secondary school. These include:

- moving to a bigger school, and not knowing who people are or how things work

- moving around the school for lessons

- meeting a wider range of peers

- increasing amounts and frequency of homework

- having different teachers for different subjects

- going from being the biggest and oldest at school, to being the smallest and youngest.

The little work that has been done on the transition demonstrates its importance to children and their families. Research undertaken by

Zeedyk and colleagues (2003), for example, confirmed the wide-ranging anxieties that children feel at this time, reflecting many of the issues listed above.

However, the changes listed above are practical and tangible ones – i.e. new environments, new ways of organising and managing time and involvement with new adults and peer groups. There are also, of course, less tangible aspects of the transition, which impact on children socially and psychologically – i.e. new challenges, demands and expectations. Whilst the transition to secondary school is a natural and inevitable part of almost all children's lives, it is also a time of considerable personal and social change for children. It is these more personal and psychological aspects of the transition that we know least about.

A key omission from much of the research and policy in this area has been the views and experiences of *parents*, and the role of parents in supporting their children at this time. For parents, their child's move from primary to secondary school can be both an exciting and a worrying time. The excitement relates to children growing up and moving into young adulthood. However, it can also be a time of anxiety for parents. Moving to secondary school signifies a change for parents in their relationship with their children and the consideration of new issues such as the changes of puberty, the increasing influence of the peer group, developments in personal relationships and sexuality, and possible use of alcohol and substances (see for example Franklin and Madge 2000; Zeedyk *et al.* 2003).

Significantly in this respect, Zeedyk and colleagues (2003, p.78) conclude from their study that parents are a key factor in their children's successful transition:

> Most research has focussed on children's fears, but the present data suggest that more attention may need to be given to parents...if a parent becomes aware of a child's concerns, they may well come to share them, and vice versa.

The Trust for the Study of Adolescence's (TSA's) review of transition projects (see Chapter 6) found that very few of the projects were focused on parents. Many of the project workers were enthusiastic about working more directly with parents. However, they were not always sure what parents needed in terms of information or support. All were certain that parents were important, though, in providing support to children. One teacher commented to the authors that parents are the 'missing piece of the jigsaw' in relation to the transition, i.e. that children and teachers/ schools need parental support and input. It is this which the research in this chapter aimed to explore.

Aims and methods of the study

The research questions were as follows:

- What are parents' experiences of parenting 9- to 11-year-olds? How do they see the parent–child relationship changing or developing during the transition to secondary school?

- What are parents' views, expectations and concerns about their child's move to secondary school?

- What information, advice and support do children and parents receive at this time, in relation to the transition?

- What more (if anything) would parents like, and in what format(s)?

In designing the study, we considered it important to involve two groups of parents – those who had children in Year 6 (i.e. whose children were about to make the transition; 10- to 11-year olds), and those who had children in Year 7 (i.e. whose children had recently made the transition; 11- to 12-year olds). There were two main stages to the research, as follows:

Stage 1: Focus groups with children: We spoke to Year 6 and Year 7 children at the start of the study, in order to inform the main part of the research with parents. Four focus groups were held with a diverse range of children in order to explore their views about the transition to secondary school and the role of parents in this. The information from these focus groups was fed into the design of the main research (see below), in relation to content, topics and language.

Stage 2: Individual interviews with parents: In total, 58 parents were individually interviewed in the study. Of this group, 16 were parents of Year 6 pupils and 42 were parents of Year 7 pupils. Interviews were conducted in parents' homes and were tape recorded. The following topics were covered:

Year 6 parents:

- their relationship with their child and whether they felt it would change in the next year (and if so how)
- how they thought their child's move to secondary school would go and what concerns they had (if any)
- what information and advice they had received about the transition so far and what else they wanted (if anything).

Year 7 parents:

- their relationship with their child and any changes that occurred during/after the move to secondary school
- how the move to secondary school had gone
- what information, advice and support they had sought or received prior to the transition
- what else, if anything, they wanted.

The sample of parents involved in the research was diverse and included 45 mothers and 13 fathers. Parents were from a range of family types, including two-parent, single-parent and step-families. The families were mainly from disadvantaged backgrounds. Parents were also diverse in terms of culture and ethnicity, with 40 of the 58 parents (69%) describing themselves as 'white British' and 18 parents (31%) describing themselves as Indian, Pakistani or African Caribbean. A small number of interviews were conducted in Urdu and then translated.

The main results of the research are described in the following section.

Parents' needs and experiences when their children move to secondary school

This section summarises the results of the study. It is divided as follows:

- parenting 9- to 11-year-olds
- anticipating the move to secondary school

- information and support activities in Year 6
- experiences of the transition
- information and support needs of parents.

Findings (1): Parenting 9- to 11-year-olds

There were three key themes that emerged in relation to participants' experiences of parenting 9- to 11-year-olds. These concerned developmental changes in the child in the last few years, recent changes in the parent–child relationship, and ease and difficulty in parenting 9- to 11-year-olds. These are explored further below.

First, the majority of the parents, whether they had Year 6 or Year 7 children, described their child as having changed in the last few years. This was seen as a natural and inevitable part of children's continuing development and something that they had expected to occur.

Most parents started by talking about the physical changes that had (and were) occurring in their children. They described how their children were starting or approaching puberty, in terms of getting taller or 'filling out'. For example:

> It's happened quite quickly. He's shot up, filled out, looks more like a young man than a boy, sort of thing. (Year 7 mother, Huddersfield)

Parents also described their children's physical change in terms of their appearance or image and a greater concern about personal hygiene. As these parents explained it:

> ...she brushes her teeth morning and night now and she didn't used to do that, not without me prompting her. But since she started at high school she has taken a lot more care in her appearance than what she would do at primary school. (Year 7 mother, Brighton)

> Yeah. He's more hygiene conscious now. He has a bath every morning before going to school, which he never used to. (Year 7 mother, Huddersfield)

In addition to physical changes, parents talked about behavioural changes in their children over the last few years. Many parents talked about children spending more time alone, or with friends. For example:

> She wants to go out with her friends a lot more now that she's older. We don't really see her much now when it's the holidays. She's goes around to friend's houses, she's round there again tonight. (Year 6 mother, Huddersfield)

Parents also commented on changes in physical behaviour, such as children becoming more assertive, and occasionally more aggressive. Other parents described their children as having become more responsible, in terms of being able to go out alone and taking more responsibility in their lives. This was often reported by parents in mixed ways – i.e. that whilst it is good that children become more independent as they get older, they can also be rude or argumentative with parents. For example, as these parents described it:

> ...she's got a hell of a lot more sarcastic. (Year 6 mother, Brighton)

> ...and I think, along those lines, that has made her more assertive. And more, I'd say, you know, getting a bit lippy and all that stuff. But I just take that as part of growing up and stuff. (Year 7 mother, Brighton)

Parents also reported that their children had changed emotionally in the last few years. Many described their child's better understanding of others, and growing emotional maturity. For example:

> I think the other thing is, she's, she's kind of, very sensitive as well, (um) and I've noticed how she's got a bit tougher. (Year 6 father, Brighton)

Second, the parents described how their relationships with their children had changed over the last few years. These changes related to their child's new relationships with friends and peers and changes in independence and monitoring. Parents said that their child was spending more time with friends and/or outside of the home and this meant that the parent saw less of them. For example:

> …one of the hard things for me is that she's going to want to go out now and do things with friends, stuff like that. Whereas before she wasn't really bothered about what happened to her on a weekend. You know, I work every other weekend, so every other weekend we all do something together, but (um) just recently I'm finding that she's saying, 'oh some of my friends are going swimming or going to the town, can I go to the town…?' (Year 7 mother, Brighton)

Another theme that emerged was that of greater responsibility and independence. Parents of the Year 7 children in particular, commented on how the transition to secondary school offered a new opportunity to give more responsibility to their child. Comments often centred around encouraging the child to 'stand on their own feet', to accept responsibility and to deal with issues and problems on their own. For example:

> I'm trying to stop mummying him and stop, make him sort of stand on his own two feet – and be more independent and stop picking everything up for him and packing his bag and 'have you got this?'. I'm trying to step back and sort of let him take a little bit of responsibility for himself… (Year 7 mother, Brighton)

Children's growing independence was closely related to changes in parental monitoring and supervision. Many parents said that they were less strict with their monitoring as their child became older, in order to give their child more independence and 'leeway'. However, a few parents indicated that they actually monitored their child more, to ensure that they were where they were supposed to be, and that they were safe. This was again more pronounced with the children who had already moved to secondary school, as parents felt less in control and were often anxious about what their children might be doing.

Finally, parents were asked about how easy or difficult it was to be the parent of a 9- to 11-year-old. The majority of parents gave a mixed response to this question, indicating that certain aspects were easier and certain aspects were more difficult. For example, parents said that the child was more responsible and able to do more things for themselves, but this was often combined with greater assertiveness. this was generally welcome, this change also often brought with it a greater amount of argumentativeness and challenging of the parent. As these parents said:

> Yeah, you have to lay down the law a bit more...like, when they're tiny, they don't think that you're wrong ever! [laughs] You'll say something and you know, they'll have a paddy and everything, but they soon get over it, and they'll do what you ask eventually – but as they get older then they, they begin to challenge things a bit more. (Year 6 mother, Hampshire)

> ...she was a very shy sort of girl but she's really come out of herself since going to big school. Sometimes she's too good at it, too mouthy [laughs]. (Year 7 mother, Brighton)

In answering this question, many parents said that it was more difficult to parent a 9- to 11-year-old than when their child was younger, because of one aspect – increased fears for their personal safety. As children got older they spent more time out of the home and with new friends and peers. As this parent explained, this often made them more concerned about their children's personal safety:

> [It's] definitely difficult now. It's not hard work like when they are young, making sure they don't touch this or that, it's more mentally harder, 'cos you do worry, every time they go out you worry where they are or what they are up to, especially in this day and age. (Year 7 mother, Huddersfield)

Findings (2): Anticipating the move to secondary school

A key section of the interviews explored what parents expected in relation to the move to secondary school. These results are summarised in this part of the chapter. They include what parents saw as the differences between primary and secondary school, how they considered their child felt about the move and their own feelings about it.

Most parents considered that primary and secondary schools were very different environments. These included:

- the size of secondary school compared to primary school
- the organisation of secondary school life, i.e. moving around for subjects, having to plan for the lessons happening each day
- no longer having one main teacher
- having to take in different books and materials each day
- the amount and difficulty of homework

- going from being the oldest and biggest child in the school, to being the youngest and smallest.

These findings did not differ between parents of Year 6 and Year 7 children. For example:

> ...it must feel really different because in primary you can just run about, run in the playground and you've never got to watch your bag. In secondary it must be like a bodyguard, you've got to be everywhere. (Year 7 mother, Brighton)

> It's up to them to sort out if they put money on the lunch card and all of that, all of this sort of complicated little responsibilities that they have to figure out to survive up there that they don't at primary school. (Year 6 mother, Brighton)

Many of the parents were also very aware of the fact that there would be much less *parental* involvement with secondary school in comparison to primary school. This applied both to the amount of involvement they felt that they would have with other parents, as well as with teachers and school activities. The issue of reduced parental involvement with their child's secondary school was a major concern about the transition for many parents. This important issue is returned to later in the chapter. Next, we turn to how parents thought their child felt (or had felt) about the transition.

Parents were asked how they thought their child was feeling about the move (for Year 6 parents), or how the parents of the Year 7 children remembered their son or daughter feeling at that time. The majority of parents felt that their child was looking forward to (or had looked forward to) the move. This was because of particular subjects they were interested in or looking forward to, getting a new uniform, having particular school facilities, or making new friends. In addition, children were described as feeling 'more grown-up' as a result of moving up to the secondary system. As these parents explained it:

> He was happy – we took him there for the day, and he was absolutely ecstatic about it. (Year 7 mother, Brighton)

> He was excited, I think, that he was leaving his juniors because they're all little children. (Year 7 mother, Brighton)

Many parents, however, also described their child as having (or having had) worries and anxieties about the move. The reasons given included anxieties about the size of the school (getting lost, etc.), meeting new people, and general uncertainties about the future. As these mothers described it:

> The size...the older children there, are a bit daunting... worried about getting lost... I think they do worry, and they hear such awful things don't they, like bullying. (Year 7 mother, Brighton)

> Just generally, what will happen, what will it be like, will I be OK, that sort of thing. (Year 6 mother, Brighton)

Overall, the parents described their child's 'mixed feelings' about the move to secondary school. The parents saw their child as having both positive views about the move and anxieties and concerns. As this mother said:

> She's got very good friends in the Year 6 and she says leaving those friends behind will be difficult, and she's not looking forward to that (um) she says she's got sort of, mixed feelings really – a bit of excitement and a bit of feeling a bit nervous about it. (Year 6 mother, Cornwall)

We also asked parents about the specific concerns that their children had about the transition. The main ones that were reported by parents included:

- concerns about travel arrangements (for example, having to get a bus for the first time, or having to change buses)
- worries about new social relationships (both with peers and teachers)
- concerns about schoolwork/homework (both the amount and difficulty)
- worries about the change in general, and whether they will experience problems such as being bullied.

In addition to asking parents about how their child felt about the move, we also explored parents' own areas of concern. A number of areas were identified, including the increased size of the school, that there are different teachers for different subjects and the fact that second-ary schools tend to place responsibility for problem-solving with the children (rather than parents). This parent, for example, represented many parents' anxieties about the level of work and homework:

> It's very different. She's got 20 minutes homework a week at the moment. So it, the, the shock is gonna be enormous isn't it? You know, for somebody who hates change. (Year 6 mother, Brighton)

Further, some parents felt that the dispersion of pupils to different schools meant that they would lose their links with other parents. This could again result in less awareness of what was going on in the school. Others were concerned about whether their child would get on with new teachers and subjects:

> I suppose it's worrying knowing that your child is going from one teacher who concentrates on them and knows them to a whole load, and if there's a subject that she's currently fine in but if the teacher doesn't get on with her then she might drop back in it, so that's a bit of a worry. (Year 6 mother, Brighton)

Some parents had more general concerns about their child settling in and getting on with other children. For example:

> I'm frightened about her getting left behind, y'know? You know, that she'll get there, she'll be totally bewildered, get completely left behind, and get in with the naughty kids and blow it. (Year 6 mother, Brighton)

And finally, as already stated, parents were concerned that they might not know how to help their child if necessary:

> Because you can't, you don't feel you can just go in there and sort things out. They have to do it themselves. You feel that they, and I think that they've got to learn that. I think there's a big transformation. (Year 7 father, Brighton)

Findings (3): Information and support activities in Year 6

This part of the section details the information that parents received, and the activities that took place, in relation to preparing for the transition. It was notable that most of the parents were unsure about the information they had received, or when they had received it, in relation to the transition. Where parents did remember receiving something, there was little consistency, and different schools/local education authorities had provided very different types and amounts of information. However, the following information was received, some aimed at children and some aimed at parents.

Information received via primary school was:

- a parent newsletter, which included advertising of open evenings at local secondary schools

- a school preference form, which included a booklet with basic facts about local schools (exam results, facilities, number on roll)

- a letter outlining the selection process and who to contact at local secondary schools

- a pack with a booklet outlining the times when parents can visit the schools

- verbal information provided by primary teachers (explaining the suitability of schools for the child in question).

Information received via secondary school was:

- a folder with '101 tips for parents', containing facts about teachers, start times and aims of the school

- a school brochure or prospectus, which contained information about teachers, the school council, map and exam results

- information sheets outlining rules and regulations, travel arrangements and uniforms (provided with confirmation of school)

- a booklet outlining the school's anti-bullying policy, travel arrangements and contact numbers

- the school plan, which lists sporting and academic achievements, information about what will be offered to Year 7 pupils and details of uniform requirements

- a pamphlet outlining the curriculum, what is expected of the pupils and what parents can do to support pupils.

In general, parents found this written information helpful, although none was considered to have provided all the information that they or their children wanted.

Many parents also reported trying to get information about secondary school from other sources, in addition to those that were sent to them. These included:

- friends and family
- other parents
- the internet
- the local education authority
- charities and voluntary organisations
- local newspapers.

It is notable that seven of the 58 parents said that they had received no information at all about their child's move to secondary school. These parents felt particularly uninformed and unsupported. Several of these were parents of children with special needs, often where parents had concerns about the emotional needs of their child. These parents felt, in particular, that basic information about secondary school was inadequate for their needs. As this parent explained it:

> I didn't get any information really about how the child would cope or anything like that. It was just on the school policies, and stuff like that really. It wasn't, you know, that he, your son, he could change, going up to high school, stuff like that. There was nothing like that. (Year 7 mother, Brighton)

Findings (4): Experiences of the transition

In the interviews we asked the Year 7 parents about how their child's move to secondary school had gone and what advice they would give to a Year 6 parent. Their responses to the first question often reflected how the parent felt their child was adjusting to growing up in general and what the child's personality was. As these parents described it:

It's been alright hasn't it. It's just been a few [issues], but that isn't school, that's her personality-wise changing. (Year 7 mother, Huddersfield)

The transition was smooth, simple and there weren't any problems. I guess I'm lucky, because she's just sailed through and got on with it, so in a way I am lucky because that's just my daughter's character and personality, that's what she'll do. (Year 7 mother, Brighton)

Parents also reported a smooth transition when they had a positive view of the secondary school in general. As mentioned earlier, many parents expressed concerns that they would not be as involved in their child's education at secondary level and would not be able to help them in the same way they could at primary school. Therefore, the schools that were seen as supportive in that respect were often mentioned by parents in very glowing terms. As these parents explained it:

Very good, yeah, very smooth. The staff, the teachers and everybody there are very helpful at helping to settle them in with just the right amount of care and concern, if you like, because I think like too much is a bad thing and they're like (um) asking, I think in the first couple of weeks you know there were people dotted around the school, you know, older children, that were there for the purpose to help the new ones to their lessons. (Year 7 mother, Brighton)

A small number of parents, however, did report a difficult transition for their child. The most commonly cited reasons were social problems, such as not fitting in, not making friends easily or being a target for bullies. Generally the change in established routine seemed to be the most unsettling for the child. As this parent explained it:

...the first three months I'd say it was difficult, to the point where I think it was just different kinds of teachers were coming in, and when he gets used to a teacher he's fine, but if a new one comes in the middle, 'cos he got two different teachers in the first three or four months...'cos the new teacher would give, like a different, not the same as the other teacher, it's different instructions or different ways of doing things, and in the middle of when he just got used to doing it and then they'll change it, you know what I mean? (Year 7 mother, Huddersfield)

Second, the Year 7 parents were asked what information and advice they would want to provide for Year 6 parents. The most common areas of advice were as follows:

Getting to know the school and teachers: Many parents felt that it was important to try and make contact with the school before their child started. This might involve, for example, attending Open Days, or speaking to Year 7 teachers. It was important, parents felt, for them to be familiar with how the school worked and the teachers/lessons that their child might have. As this parent explained it:

> ...to know who they'll have for what, how things work. It does help. (Year 7 mother, Brighton)

Communicating with and supporting the child: Many parents talked about the importance of encouraging an open dialogue with children about the transition, and reassuring them. For example, as this parent described it:

> When they start they need to be reassured that they are going to be okay...they need lots of reassurance as it is such a big thing. (Year 7 mother, Brighton)

This point was linked to parents' comments (highlighted earlier) about the anxieties that many children had that were 'bubbling beneath the surface'.

Taking 'a back seat': When talking about advice for Year 6 parents, a very common phrase used was 'taking a back seat'. Many advised that parents should let their children develop independence and responsibility, so that they are more mentally prepared for the transition. As this father explained:

> Once they go into a secondary school you can't...they've got to look after themselves more. That's part of learning, and it's part of life. It's one of those things that, a stage they've moved on to isn't it? (Year 7 father, Brighton)

It should also be acknowledged that most parents said this was often quite difficult in practice. Parents said that when their child had a problem, their instinct was to try and sort it out for them. They stressed, however, that part of growing up was to encourage children to deal with their own problems and difficulties.

Doing basic preparation: Many parents felt that getting the practical things prepared contributed to a smooth transition. This meant things like travel arrangements, uniform, equipment needed and materials. As this parent explained it:

> Well, travelling's quite difficult if they've got a long distance to travel and make sure you take them on the journey more than once, just to make sure you know they definitely know what bus to get on at what stop, where to get off and where to get on the next one... (Year 7 mother, Brighton)

Other parents, in relation to this, explained how they telephoned the school, or asked other parents, for information on what equipment or materials to take. This, parents said, helped to reassure children that they had everything that they needed in the first few days.

Findings (5): Information and support needs of parents

Most of the parents felt that there was more information and support that they would like. There was a wide range of information that parents wanted and this fell into four broad categories:

- practical information
- school bullying policies and procedures
- school facts and information about extra-curricular activities
- special needs provision.

What parents wanted within each of these areas is detailed in turn below:

PRACTICAL INFORMATION

Almost all the parents felt they needed more information about the practical aspects of the move to secondary school. These included answers to questions such as: where do they get the uniform from, what pens or books should they buy, how is lunch organised, what is needed for PE (physical education) classes? Parents said that they wanted this information both for themselves and for their child. Having clear information about these things – and in particular having it in advance – was important for helping children to prepare for the move and to feel confident in their first few days. For example:

> It is important for them, knowing what to take, pens, books and that…it does help them to feel more confident… (Year 7 mother, Huddersfield)

Travel arrangements to and from school, however, was the key area of practical information that parents wanted more information about. This was because it often involved a change of routine for their child (for example, getting up earlier in order to catch the bus) and raised safety issues (i.e. travelling alone for the first time). It also involved practical issues that parents often did not know the answer to – for example whether there are any special school buses, when and where they go from, how much it costs, etc. As this mother explained it:

> There wasn't, there wasn't really any, any information about how to get to school…that would have been better, for example I had to find out myself where the school bus leaves from and, and that, that kind of stuff, (um), so, no we weren't told any of that actually…because that would have been better – if, if I had already known and could, would have been able to tell [N], you know the school bus just leaves from right from round the corner from here and goes right to the school – but we didn't know any of that until a few days before we, before she started. (Year 7 mother, Brighton)

It is unclear whether travel arrangements are a particular concern for most parents of transition-age pupils, or whether this sample had a particular concern about it. However, it repeatedly came up as something that parents wanted more information about and preparation for. This was mainly because arriving late at school, and thus missing registration and/or getting into trouble, was a particular cause for concern for children.

SCHOOL BULLYING POLICIES AND PROCEDURES

Many parents referred to bullying as something that they (and their children) were concerned about. Their anxieties were heightened because of media stories about bullying and anecdotal stories from other parents. Many also said that being bullied was one of their children's greatest fears about secondary school. One Year 6 parents described her fears for her daughter in this respect:

> I am worried about bullying. Not because I think she is particularly a subject for it, but I don't think that she is particularly not either. She stands out for a number of reasons, and sometimes that's all it takes. (Year 6 mother, Brighton)

As a result, many parents in the study said that they wanted information about bullying. This included knowing how the school dealt with bullying, i.e. what was their policy about it and how incidents were managed. Parents also wanted to know who they should speak to if they were concerned about this and what actions might then be taken as a result. In particular, many parents wanted to have this information in order to talk things through with their child. This, parents felt, would reassure their child, and help the parent and child to deal with any bullying that did occur.

SCHOOL FACTS AND INFORMATION ABOUT EXTRA-CURRICULAR ACTIVITIES

Parents also wanted information about school facts and extra-curricular activities. These two areas were closely related as they both centred around understanding the school better and making the most of what it had to offer. This information was particularly important when parents were looking at schools during the selection process, as well as when they knew which school their child was going to be going to.

It was important to have this information, parents said, to help children to settle in and to take advantage of any opportunities given. Many parents indicated that the process of transition was stressful enough, so having more accessible information about schools helped ease the process. As this parent explained it:

> Yeah I think [school] are quite good, they have...a kind of, weekly staff newsletter, 'cos I've seen a couple them. They're really informative, honest you know, really, really helpful and as a teacher I found them really helpful but I think that gives a kind of accurate, more like a flavour of what goes on 'cos they're not about marketing the school so something like...'cos you know, you, you're getting a sense of what the staff on the

team…what kind of communication structures there are, I'd, I'd find that kind of, quite valuable… (Year 6 father, Brighton)

Another key area that parents wanted more information about was extra-curricular activities. As these mothers explained it:

It is important, what clubs and things there are to do, makes them, you know, look forward to what's on offer. (Year 6 mother, Brighton)

Yeah, I mean, they have an awful lot of after-school clubs, which I think is really good and they tell the children about them… (Year 6 mother, Hampshire)

This parent continued by saying that if parents knew about the extra-curricular activities and clubs available, they could help their children to get involved. This might help them to settle in, make new friends and learn new skills or hobbies.

SPECIAL NEEDS PROVISION

The final key area that many parents wanted more information about was special needs. This applied to a significant proportion of families in the study and has already been highlighted a number of times in this chapter. The information and support required in relation to special needs covered a number of different areas. First, parents wanted more information to help them to select schools. For example, as this parent of a Year 6 child with special needs said:

I've been round to a few schools obviously, but I've found it quite hard to get information. I must admit…because he has special needs and where they all have, it's all going out to find it myself, but it still hasn't been that easy… Well, I could, definitely could have, could be a bit more information on the special needs sort of side of the education. (Year 6 mother, Brighton)

Other parents whose children were already at secondary school also felt that they needed more information and support. For example:

…they've [the secondary school] been saying he has got special needs and they should be catering for his special needs. (Year 7 mother, Huddersfield)

...but if you know your child is very able, you would hope that, that, I mean, if they say, oh yes, well we, you know, we deal with special needs and we have enough resources for that. (Year 6 mother, Brighton)

It should be stressed that, throughout this study, parents of children with special needs made a particular point of having information and support during the transition. This was to help them as parents and to enable them to help and support their children.

Conclusions and recommendations

The research described in this chapter explored a key issue within social policy and in the lives of children and families – the transition to secondary school. In particular, the study focused on what has been described as the 'missing piece of the jigsaw' – the needs and experiences of *parents* during their child's move to secondary school. A wide range of needs and issues was identified, and parents felt that meeting these needs and addressing the issues would help them to support their children at this key transition point. A number of policy and practice recommendations therefore arise from this study. These are as follows:

- A key issue raised by the findings is whether more can be done in *primary* schools to help prepare children for the move to secondary school. Many parents felt that their children were looking forward to the move, but that they might be underestimating the amount of change and difficulty they would experience. This was because, parents felt, primary schools were not doing enough to prepare children for the realities of life in secondary school. Preparation might include, for example, group discussions, standardised information packs and visits to primary schools by Year 7 pupils. In particular, it is considered important to balance the positive and encouraging information given to children with an acknowledgement of the difficulties and challenges they might face.

- Most parents in this study wanted more information and support about the transition, in order to help them to feel prepared and to help their children. Most parents in this study wanted more information to read at home – this could be leaflets, packs, fliers or newsletters. It is of note that newsletters for parents has been shown by other TSA research to be a format particularly valued by parents (see Chapter 8). The TSA has recently produced some newsletter-style information for parents on the move to secondary school.

- One group of parents in the study found the transition a particularly difficult time – parents of children with special needs. It is important that this group of parents has extra help, at an early stage, in relation to decision making about choice of school. In addition, these parents require more detailed information and support in relation to the particular special needs of their child – whether in terms of disability, learning support or behavioural issues.

- It was also clear in this study that some children with certain characteristics might find the move to secondary school particularly difficult – children who parents described as shy, or withdrawn, or who had difficulty making friends. Some parents also felt that certain things about their child (such as being overweight or not very good at school work) could make them a 'target' for bullying. These children, parents considered, needed extra help and support during the move to secondary school. It is of note that TSA has recently finished an evaluation of a pilot project, which is doing just this. It worked with the National Pyramid Trust (NPT), which runs 'Pyramid Clubs' in primary schools. These clubs take place over ten weeks, for children who are identified by parents, teachers and other school staff as particularly withdrawn and shy and who have difficulty making friends. The children are identified as those who might find the move to secondary school particularly difficult. This model could be implemented elsewhere.

- A key finding from the study was that many parents felt 'distanced' from secondary school, compared to primary school. This was because they did not have the single teacher that they had had in each year of primary school who they could approach with any issues or concerns about their child. It would be useful for secondary schools to have one nominated person who Year 7 parents can contact about their child. Whilst it is acknowledged that some schools do already do this, even where schools in this study had this procedure, many parents were not aware of this. More needs to be done, therefore, to help parents to access help from a named person when their children are in Year 7. Getting parents involved in the school at this time, and helping them to understand the processes involved, may keep them engaged throughout their child's time at the school.

It is considered that, if these changes are implemented, parents will be much more supported in relation to the move to secondary school. Parents will therefore be in a position to help and support their children at this crucial time.

Learning for practitioners

- Most parents of 9- to 11-year-olds notice considerable change in their children during this time. Many want more information and support. Projects to support parents of 'pre-teens', particularly around the move to secondary school, would be valued by parents.

- Many parents feel that they lack information about how secondary schools 'work' – more details are needed so that parents can understand terminology, structure, key staff, etc.

- Most parents want more information and support in relation to their child's move to secondary school. They particularly want information about four topics – practical information, school facts and procedures, bullying policies and procedures, and special needs.

- Parents want information about the transition to be provided in a variety of ways. This includes leaflets, information sheets and newsletters.

- Parents also want more information about the realities of the move to secondary school for their children. Staff in primary schools and those working with this age group may want to balance the positive features presented about secondary school with information about the realities of secondary school life.

References

Christensen, P., James, A., Jenks, C. and McNamee, S. (1999) *'Changing Times' Project*. Hull: University of Hull.

Franklin, A. and Madge, N. (2000) *Paths to Progress: The Transition from Primary to Secondary School in the London Borough of Waltham Forest*. London: National Children's Bureau.

Galton, M., Gray, J. and Ruddock, J. (1999) *The Impact of School Transition and Transfer on Pupil Progress and Attainment*. Research Report. London: Department for Education and Employment.

Tabor, D. (1993) 'Smoothing their path: transition, continuity and pastoral liaison between primary and secondary school.' *Pastoral Care in Education 11*, 1, 10–14.

Zeedyk, S., Gallacher, J., Henderson, M., Hope, G., Husband, B. and Lindsay, K. (2003) 'Negotiating the transition from primary to secondary school: perceptions of pupils, parents and teachers.' *School Psychology International 24*, 1, 67–79.

6 Supporting children and parents during the transition to secondary school: A UK-wide review

Debi Roker and Julie Shepherd

Background to the project

Children's transition from primary to secondary school is a key issue for researchers, practitioners and policy-makers (see Chapter 5 for further information). A growing body of literature is now available, which demonstrates the wide range of new experiences that children face at this time. Amongst the many changes involved, children go from being the oldest to the youngest in their school, move around for lessons, have a number of different teachers instead of one and start to be given increased amounts of homework.

The literature on this topic shows that many children have mixed views about the transition, feeling both positive and excited, and anxious, at the same time. We also know that whilst for most children the transition is a smooth one, many other children find it difficult and problematic (DfES 2003; Galton and Morrison 2000; Marks 2004; Zeedyk et al. 2003). Anecdotal evidence also suggests that many practitioners identify the transition to secondary school as a key intervention point, with a link to later risk-taking and exclusion. Research shows that many children experience a dip in academic performance by the time they reach Year 8, i.e. after they have been at secondary school for a year (Galton, Gray and Ruddock 1999). Finally, the literature demonstrates that the transition to secondary school is also a key time for parents, with little information and support available to them at this time (for further details see Chapter 5).

During the last few years, the Trust for the Study of Adolescence (TSA) has become aware of an increase in the number of projects and interventions that are designed to support children and/or parents during the transition to secondary school. Many of these were innovative and exciting and aimed to support both children and parents through the transition. Crucially, they aimed to address many of the issues identified in the literature outlined above – children's and parents' anxieties, academic continuity and performance, the need for social and emotional support at times of change, etc. It became clear to us, however, that many of these projects were only known about in local areas, and there was considerable 'reinventing of the wheel'. TSA therefore decided to undertake a UK-wide review of transition projects. The results of this review are detailed in this chapter. The aim of the review was to find out what types of projects are in existence, what their objectives are, how they are funded and what issues they face in providing transition support to children and/or parents.

Methods used in the review

The review was undertaken during 2002 and 2003. There were two main stages to the project, as follows.

First, we produced a flier, requesting information about any projects or initiatives that aimed to support children and/or parents during the transition to secondary school. This flier was sent to a very wide range of local and national organisations, representing schools, the youth service, social services and a range of statutory and voluntary bodies. In total, 199 fliers were returned.

Second, all of these projects were then either sent a self-completion questionnaire or interviewed over the telephone. The questions asked in the two methods were the same. The areas explored were as follows:

- the history of the project
- the aim of the project
- the type of project or activity
- the numbers of children and/or parents reached

- funding for the work
- how long the project has been underway
- staffing of the project
- any training and support issues
- other issues faced by the project providers.

In total, completed questionnaires or telephone interviews were completed with practitioners from 125 projects. The projects represented all four countries of the UK, although the greatest number of participating projects were located in Scotland, the south-east and the north-west.

A range of organisations took part in the review. These included schools, counselling services, parent support projects, children and young people's projects, local education authorities (LEAs), family centres, special educational needs organisations and education initiatives. Children and young people's projects were by far the most common organisations who took part, making up almost a third of the responses. This was followed by LEAs, which made up just under a fifth, followed by parent support projects and education initiatives, both of which consisted of a tenth. Further information about the projects that responded is given below, with main responses summarised, and some quotes used to illustrate the points made.

Main findings
Aims of the projects

Most of the 125 projects had a diverse range of aims. The three most common aims were to promote a smooth personal/emotional transition for children (34% of total responses), to promote a smooth curriculum/academic transition (15% of responses) and to improve children's confidence and self-esteem around the transition (15%).

Types of support offered

Half of the 125 projects were what we call in this chapter 'general support' projects, which included a focus on the transition period *as part of* the projects' work with families. The remaining half were specific 'transition-focused' projects, focused *solely* on providing support during the transition to secondary school. Over 60 per cent of the projects provided support to children and parents, 34 per cent to children only, and 6 per cent to parents only. Here are three examples of the sort of work that was being done:

- *'Transition-focused' projects for children and parents*: One project took place in a family centre, based near Edinburgh. It was based in a school and focused specifically on the transition. It offered one-to-one work and groupwork, and also provided written information. It was targeted in particular at children who the teacher felt need additional support. The support started after Easter, with some contact provided during the summer holidays. Children then had contact with the project during the first year of secondary school. Leaflets were also produced for teachers and parents, and support for parents of these children was also available.

- *'Transition-focused' projects just for children*: Another project was a crime reduction/early intervention project based in Cornwall, which worked only with children. It provided class work and a two-day workshop for all children, but also targeted groupwork with children who have low self-esteem. All of this work took place in the summer term of Year 6, prior to the move to secondary school.

- *'Transition-focused' projects just for parents*: One of the projects was based in Derbyshire, focusing on parents in rural areas. This project involved researching the needs of parents during the transition and then producing materials and services to address these issues. The findings were used to produce a booklet for parents, and a 'parenting teenagers' course. The research showed that parents' concerns were: bullying, the journey to school, finding the way around school and tackling the work. These concerns were reflected in the booklet and the course.

Types of activity undertaken

The types of activity provided within the projects were extremely variable, with many offering more than one type. The four main types of support provided were: information and materials (23% of responses), groupwork (20% of responses), one-to-one help and support (19% of responses) and organised visits to secondary schools (15% of responses). In addition, some projects offered summer camps and activities, home visits, mentoring and peer support. Here is an example of a peer support project:

- This project is based in the north-west and focuses specifically on the transition period. The main part of the project is to offer peer support. All children in Year 6 take part in a workshop, which aims to identify their hopes and fears. Pupils in Year 10 are trained as peer supporters, to help the new Year 7 pupils overcome their fears and realise their hopes. Bullying and racism were identified as the main fears for the Year 6 children. This project takes place in six secondary schools and 18 primary schools in the local area.

Whether projects are open to all or targeted

In total, 50 per cent of the projects were open to any child/parent who wished to take part and 50% were targeted at certain groups or limited to particular groups. Of those projects which were targeted, most of these were aimed at children who it was thought were at risk of finding the transition difficult. The remainder of targeted projects were mainly focused on children with special educational needs or on parents who were experiencing particular difficulties themselves or in their relationship with their children.

Longevity of projects

Most of the projects had not been in existence for very long. One-third had been running for five years or more, with another third only having started the year before. The projects focusing on the transition specifically (rather than those providing general support that included a transition element) were much more likely to have been set up recently.

Those running projects in collaboration with other services

A wide range of organisations was involved in running the projects in the review, including schools, LEAs, educational bodies and statutory and voluntary bodies. Two-thirds of the projects said that they ran their project in collaboration with other organisations. The most common collaborators were schools (18% of responses), community-based projects (13%), social services (13%), community health (13%) and LEAs (12%). Many projects were running as partnerships between a wide range of organisations.

Funding of the projects

The majority of the projects (88%) had specific funding for their work. These projects were funded by a range of agencies, including the Children's Fund, the Department for Education and Skills, Barnardos and LEAs. Many of the projects received support from more than one funder. There was also a difference between the projects in terms of the longevity of their funding. In total, 39 per cent of the projects received ongoing funding, 29 per cent had time-limited or project-specific funding and 19 per cent received occasional or one-off funding. The remaining projects received their funding in other ways. Funding for their work was a key issue for all of the projects. It arose repeatedly in terms of the range of current activities they were able to provide and the extent to which they were able to offer and plan new services. The issue of funding for projects is a key issue and is returned to in later sections of this chapter.

Length of the projects

There was considerable variety in the period that the projects focused on. Just under half of the projects started in Year 6 and continued into Year 7, with 17 per cent taking place in the summer term of Year 6 only. Other projects took place at variable times, or were one-off events.

Whether projects extend past the transition period

We explored with projects whether they had 'one-off' or ongoing contact with the users of their projects. Just over half of the projects (55%) had informal contact with the users of the project or programme once it had come to an end. A fifth (22%) had formal contact with the users and a quarter (24%) had no contact with users at all.

There were some differences between the 'transition-focused' projects and the 'general support' projects in this respect. The 'transition-focused' projects were much more likely to have more *informal* contact once the project came to an end, and the 'general support' projects much more likely to have *formal* contact with project users. Here is what some projects said about follow-up contact:

> Siblings coming through the system is the usual point of contact – although we find parents increasingly able to cope following first intervention. Some also keep in touch at times of later crisis when a suitable referral is made elsewhere.

> Only informally at the moment, but we have to formalise it this year.

> Yes, they're always welcome to come back to us.

> We are tracking them and providing support in the high school.

In concluding this section, it should be stressed that the majority of the projects did not have ongoing contact with children or parents after the transition period. Whilst many projects wanted to be able to provide ongoing support, lack of funds and resources meant they usually had to 'move on' to another group.

Materials used in transition projects

The majority of the projects in the review (78%) used materials of some kind in their work. These included a specific book, programme or video (40% of responses), materials or resources produced by the project itself (38%), or materials produced by the Qualifications and Curriculum Authority (QCA) or as part of the National Curriculum (7%). In terms of these materials, there was a very wide range of resources being used, and no one material was used more commonly than any other.

Monitoring and evaluation of projects

Two-thirds of the projects said that they collected information about those who used their projects, including the social background, gender and ethnicity of users. The vast majority of the projects also stated that they had monitoring or evaluation procedures in place to judge the success of their work. Just over a third of the projects (38%) said that they had developed their own system of evaluation. Others used monitoring systems such as having external evaluators, and systems developed by Ofsted and Best Value.

As might be expected, most project workers felt that their work did have an impact on parents' and children's experiences of the transition. Here are some examples:

> Children feel more confident and secure. We are listening to their fears and taking them seriously and providing support.

> Parents – hopefully they will become more involved in school and child's education if we can remove barriers.

> Excellent, the children have been able to negotiate the transition really well.

> It gave the children a member of staff they could approach if they had worries.

> We aim to encourage families to problem-solve themselves – in order to prevent difficulties spiralling.

Despite these positive comments, it should be stressed that most projects had not been formally evaluated. However, most project workers were convinced about the effectiveness of their work and were keen to do a formal evaluation if the financial support for this was provided.

Hard-to-reach groups

Just under half of the respondents (45%) said that their project did have some children or parents who were hard to reach. The most commonly mentioned groups were vulnerable and disadvantaged families (23%), and black and minority ethnic families (17%). In addition, projects mentioned Traveller families, families with disabled children or those with special educational needs, and non-English speaking parents.

Difficulties faced by project providers

The projects were asked whether there were any aspects that made it difficult for them to provide their transition projects. Over two-thirds of the projects (69%) replied that there were things that made it difficult for them to run their projects. The main responses were getting ongoing funding for their work (36%) (which reflects comments made earlier) and providing training and support to school or project staff (24%). Additional issues raised by some projects included: a lack of awareness or appreciation of transition issues, school staff being overwhelmed and securing parental consent for children to take part in projects.

There was a large amount of information collected in this project. Some conclusions and recommendations for policy and practice are given below.

Conclusions

The results of this UK-wide review have demonstrated, amongst other things, that there is now a burgeoning range of projects to support children and parents during the transition to secondary school. We do not claim that this survey represents all the projects taking place in the UK – clearly there are many more. However, the survey does demonstrate the growing importance of supporting children and parents through the transition to secondary school. As demonstrated in the background section of this chapter, there is a growing body of literature that high-lights the importance of the transition for both children and their parents.

A number of conclusions can be drawn from the results of the survey. These are detailed below.

The importance of supporting children and parents during the transition period

There was a clear consensus in this survey that children and parents need information and support at this key transitional point. It was significant that in this survey a large proportion of projects were new and had been set up with funding from government. This is very welcome. However, it is clear that more work needs to be undertaken in this important area, in particular because of the relevance of this time for the prevention of future risk-taking and exclusion. The transition to secondary school is now recognised as a key opportunity to support children and their families and to prepare for the adolescent period. The authors therefore believe that more attention and resources should be devoted to this period in children's lives. The emergence of extended schools makes this particularly important.

Focusing on parents

The majority of transition projects that are currently available are aimed at *children*. In this survey only 6 per cent of projects focused on information and support to *parents*. TSA's recent research into the needs of parents during their child's move to secondary school (see Chapter 5) shows that most parents want more information and support. This is to help them to understand the process, but also to help support their children at this time. Since TSA's survey (described in this chapter) was undertaken, TSA has become aware of many more projects being set up to support parents.

Supporting vulnerable children

A number of the projects in this survey were focusing on the needs of vulnerable children during the transition. This is clearly an important topic for the future. Since the completion of this survey, TSA has undertaken some further work focusing on vulnerable children and the transition. We have recently completed an evaluation of an innovative 'transition' project run by the National Pyramid Trust (NPT). This NPT project ran in a number of London primary schools and involved the identification of shy and withdrawn children, in particular those who had few friends and poor interpersonal skills. It was considered that this group of children could find the move to secondary school particularly difficult. NPT ran ten-week-long 'Pyramid Clubs' for this group, focusing on developing their interpersonal skills, building their confidence and exploring their concerns about the move to secondary school. TSA's evaluation of this project is available from the authors. The results show that this group of vulnerable children has specific needs during the transition and that interventions such as the NPT clubs can make a positive difference. Further efforts need to be made to support this group.

Funding issues

A key finding from the survey described in this chapter, is that many long-established and successful projects struggle to secure funding for their work. It is considered essential that increased funding is directed at this vital area. Many project workers were frustrated when they heard of successful and well-used projects closing down because of lack of funding, only to re-emerge a year or two later when funding was then found. By then, however, key staff and expertise had often been lost. One interesting finding was also that many of the projects and project workers were unaware of some of the funding sources available. Further dissemination about this is essential.

Research and evaluation of projects

Whilst anecdotal and preliminary evidence suggests that many of these transition projects are effective, there is little firm evaluation data available. Rigorous and long-term research is needed to establish the effectiveness of these different types of transition support projects. Such evidence would enable resources to be focused on the most successful projects and it would help those running projects to seek to extend their work using an evidence-based argument.

Networking and practice development

One clear finding from the survey is that there is insufficient information-sharing between practitioners and policy-makers in relation to the transition to secondary school. Many projects are started by organisations from scratch, with little opportunity to build on the learning from already existing projects. There is thus considerable 'reinventing of the wheel' in relation to transition support. Many workers found this particularly frustrating, as they realised that this happened. A network of practitioners and policy-makers working in this area is essential, as well as the circulation of information, ideas and evidence to those involved.

It should be mentioned that TSA is currently addressing this issue in a current project. The TSA's 'Parenting 8–11s' project is aimed at practitioners working in a range of settings. It focuses on general issues in supporting parents of 'pre-teens', with a particular focus on the transition to secondary school. This project is addressing some of the issues raised in this chapter, in particular around networking and practice development. It includes, for example, a monthly email newsletter, which shares information and ideas about projects, funding, effective work, 'hints and tips', etc. The TSA is also producing a 'Toolkit' of information and resources for use by practitioners working in this area.

In conclusion, this chapter has described the current nature of transition support across the UK, for both parents and children. The recommendations given above have emerged from this survey, and from

TSA's other work with practitioners. It is considered essential that these recommendations are acted upon in order to provide effective support to children and parents at the key transition point of the move to secondary school.

Learning for practitioners

- Little information is available about the range and nature of 'transition' support in the UK. This information is important in order to identify future needs.

- Most UK transition projects focus on the needs of children only, with relatively few involving parents. As other TSA research has shown (see Chapter 5), most parents want more information and support in relation to their children's transition.

- The balance between offering transition projects to all children and parents versus a targeted approach focusing on certain groups, was a key dilemma for workers. It is important for any new project to be clear about the reasons for providing general or targeted support services.

- Funding for projects is a key issue. There is now a wide range of potential funders of transition projects and further efforts to disseminate this knowledge is vital.

- Many projects wanted to do more detailed monitoring and supervision of their work. This evaluation, where it was undertaken, proved enormously valuable. The evaluation was used to inform the development of the work and – crucially – to also support future applications for funding.

- Networking between transition projects is an effective way of developing links, sharing expertise and developing practice. Readers are advised to contact TSA for further information about its 'Parenting 8–11s' practice development project and networks.

References

DfES (Department for Education and Skills) (2003) *Materials for Schools: Involving Parents, Raising Achievement*. London: DfES.

Galton, M. and Morrison, I. (2000) 'Transfer and transition: the next steps.' *International Journal of Educational Research, 33*, 4, 443–449.

Galton, M., Gray, J. and Ruddock, J. (1999) *The Impact of School Transitions and Transfers on Pupil Progress and Attainment*. London: DfES.

Marks, N. (2004) *The Power and Potential of Well-being Indicators*. London: New Economics Foundation.

Zeedyk, S., Gallacher, J., Henderson, M., Hope, G., Husband, B. and Lindsay, K. (2003) 'Negotiating the transition from primary to secondary school: perceptions of pupils, parents and teachers.' *School Psychology International 24*, 1, 67–79.

Part 3

New Ways of Working with Parents

7 Working with schools to support parents: lessons from two evaluations

Debi Roker and Helen Richardson Foster

This chapter focuses on an important initiative that the Trust for the Study of Adolescence (TSA) has been developing over recent years. This involves working with *schools* to provide information, advice and support for parents of young people. The TSA has undertaken two projects in this area, with two very different schools. The chapter highlights the learning from these two projects and includes the results of the evaluation into parents' views and experiences of the projects. It is structured as follows:

- background to the project
- the first school-based project – 'Fieldings' school
- the second school-based project – 'Adler' school
- conclusions: learning from the two projects.

Background
Throughout its history, TSA has explored many different ways of offering support to the parents of young people, a group of parents who have traditionally found few sources of advice and information available to them (see Chapter 1). The TSA has long been involved in the production of materials and resources for parents of teenagers (in the form of books, audiotapes and videos) and in the mid-1990s identified the rapid expansion in group-based courses for this group of parents, which have now become widespread. It also became clear at this time, however, that

there was little research-based information about the effectiveness of offering parents different types of support.

The authors were particularly interested in investigating the effectiveness of providing support on a universal basis, in settings such as schools. We undertook a brief review, speaking to a range of practitioners and policy-makers about the potential of working with schools to provide support to parents. One of the themes that came out of these discussions was that whilst many schools were providing some forms of support (for example an occasional group-based course, or a parents' Open Evening) there was little structured support available. In particular, we could find no research or projects that had worked with schools to provide *different types* of information and support. It was this that the two projects described below aimed to do.

Over a period of four years, we undertook two school-based projects to provide a range of different types of information and support to parents. These experimental projects included a detailed evaluation. Both projects had a similar design and included offering three main services to parents:

- materials – including books, leaflets, videos, etc. – for parents to use at home

- group-based courses – 8- to 12-session courses run at the schools by experienced external staff

- a Parent Adviser – an experienced family worker in place at the schools for an amount of time per week, to meet parents individually.

There were some differences in how the project was run at each school, but the basic structure of the project focused on offering these three services. All services were free and parents could use as many of the services as they wished. At both schools, the principles underlying the projects were as follows:

- Parents of young people have a right to information, advice and support in bringing up their children.

- The provision of such support can have a range of positive outcomes, including better parent–teenager relationships and a reduction in risk behaviours amongst young people.

- Such support should be offered on a universal basis, thus avoiding the targeting and stigmatising of individual parents or families.

- The support offered must be appropriate and responsive to parents' individual needs, circumstances and culture, as well as building on the strengths within families and in their relationships.

- Early support for parents, particularly those in disadvantaged communities, can prevent difficulties and possible statutory intervention later on.

Further details about each of the projects are given below. A final section of the chapter then explores some of the general issues that came out of these two projects in terms of working with schools to provide information and support to parents.

The first school-based project – 'Fieldings' school

The secondary school involved in the project (here called 'Fieldings' school) had long wanted to work more closely with parents of children at the school and offer more information and support to them. The school, located in a small town in England, was in an area of economic and social disadvantage. The school had a large number of pupils with special educational needs and a high level of exclusions and pupil turnover.

The project was both funded and supported by the local social services department, and we worked closely with both the school and the local authority in running the project. Following discussions with the school, it was agreed to run the pilot project with parents of Year 8 pupils only (i.e. parents of 12- to 13-year-olds). The parents in this year group were asking the school for information and support in large numbers and this was stretching the time and expertise of school staff. It was therefore agreed to design and offer a project to provide different types of information and support to the parents of this year group.

The three interconnected support services were offered to parents over the course of one school year. The services offered – in more detail – were as follows:

- *Materials about adolescence.* Parents were offered up to three materials, free of charge and for them to keep. These included books, videos and audiotapes on topics including: parenting teenagers, living in step-families, suicide and self-harm, sexuality, drugs and lone parenting.

- *Group-based parenting programmes.* Two courses were offered, one run in the daytime and one in the evenings. These were eight weeks long (two hours per session) and were run by experienced family workers. The courses addressed issues such as communication, conflict, negotiation, etc.

- *One-to-one support.* A Parent Adviser was appointed to provide one-to-one support to the parents in the year group. The experienced counsellor and family worker appointed to this role was available one day per week at the school (no appointment needed) and also one evening per week over the telephone.

It was considered important for both projects that a full evaluation was undertaken. All parents were approached to take part in the evaluation. At the start of the project at the Fieldings school, 102 parents from 66 families were individually interviewed. These interviews explored the nature of their parent–child relationships and any support needs that they might have. This information was used to input into the design of the services offered (above). In addition, follow-up interviews were conducted at the end of the project. In total, 80 individual interviews were undertaken at the follow-up. Parents were also asked to complete short questionnaires if they used any of the three services described above.

In total, 70 per cent of the families in the year group used at least one of the services. Of this group, 40 per cent used one service, 23 per cent used two and 7 per cent used all three. The breakdown per service was as follows:

- *Materials.* 35 families ordered a total of 111 materials. The most frequently requested materials were a *Living with Teenagers* video, and a book for parents called *Teenagers in the Family.*

- *Parenting courses.* 12 parents attended the two courses.

- *Parent Adviser.* By the start of the second term of the school year, the Parent Adviser had been contacted by 13 parents. As a result of this relatively low level of contact, the worker proactively telephoned each family in the year, to introduce herself and offer any information or support that they wanted. This was received very positively by the families. In the end the Parent Adviser spoke to 62 of the 99 families. This contact often led to discussions about parenting and parent–child relationships and/or to the provision of materials and further support.

The results of the follow-up evaluation with parents showed that the majority was extremely positive about the project. In the second round of interviews, 90 per cent of parents described the project as 'excellent' or 'very good'. Significantly, this view was expressed by parents whether they used any of the services or not. For those who had not used the services, they said it was reassuring to know that they were there if they needed them.

The more detailed results from the evaluation also showed that the project had been valuable for many parents. There were some improvements in parents' information, understanding and level of support that they felt they had, by the end of the project. For example, at the start of the project, 19 per cent of parents said they had 'no worries or concerns' about their teenager, compared to 40 per cent by the end of the project. There were other significant differences in parents' views by the end of the project. These included:

- Fewer parents wanted to significantly change their relationship with their teenager.

- More parents felt that they communicated well with their teenager.

- More parents felt that they had a good amount of knowledge about the changes of the teenage years.

Some of the issues raised by this project are addressed later in the chapter. Next, however, TSA's second school-based project is described. This was undertaken the year after the project at the Fieldings school (above) was completed. It took place in a different school, in a different area, with a different group of parents.

The second school-based project – 'Adler' school

The 'Adler' school (as it is called here) was a large community college in a rural part of England. Although the area surrounding the school was mixed in terms of social and economic factors, the families involved were from more advantaged backgrounds than at the Fieldings school. The project was run following discussions between TSA and the Adler school. The school had heard about the project run at Fieldings school, and were keen to make something similar available to parents.

Following discussions with school staff, it was decided to offer the same three pilot services. However, it was also suggested by the school that these services be offered to more than one year group. It was therefore agreed to run the pilot project with parents of young people in two year groups, Years 8 and 10. The project was therefore run for parents of young people aged 12 to 13 and 14 to 15. As before, a detailed evaluation was also undertaken. This included interviews and telephone questionnaires with parents at the start and at the end of the project, and questionnaires completed by those using each of the services. In total, 120 families were involved in the evaluation.

Overall, 88 families (23%) used at least one of the services. In total, 59 families used one service, 18 families used two, and 11 used three of the services. The services were used by parents as follows:

- *Materials*: In total, 63 families ordered one of the TSA materials. The most commonly ordered materials were the book on *Teenagers in the Family* and the video on *Living with Teenagers*. Note that in addition in this project, a small number of parents borrowed some of the materials from a resources 'library', which was set up at the school.

- *Group-based courses*: In total, five courses were run, attended by 46 individuals from 41 families. More mothers than fathers attended, with 40 women and six men participating.

- *Parent Adviser*: The Parent Adviser had 50 sessions with parents during the course of the school year. This involved 17 individual parents and two couples. Whilst some of these parents had only one or two contacts with the Parent Adviser, a few parents had up to ten contacts. Many of this latter group of parents were experiencing particular difficulties, such as a death or serious illness in the family, mental health problems, or a son/daughter refusing to attend school or being near exclusion.

- *Sessions for fathers:* During the course of the project, a number of fathers asked whether some events could be held just for fathers. As a result, two one-off sessions were held, run by an experienced external facilitator. In total, 20 fathers attended the two sessions.

The results from the interviews with parents at the beginning and end of the project revealed a number of interesting findings. Those parents who used the services were generally very positive about them and felt that it was a good thing that the school was involved in a project to support parents. Some parents reported finding the materials too simplistic. Views about the parenting courses were generally very positive, and those parents who used the Parent Adviser generally felt that they had received very good advice and support. Few differences were found on the qualitative interview measures, between the first and second interviews. A small number of differences were found, however, on some items. At the second time point, parents:

- were more confident in their ability to parent a teenager

- felt more supported in their parenting

- felt less in need of additional support

- felt more knowledgeable about the changes of the teenage years

- felt that their teenager was less concerned about what they thought of them.

It is of note, however, that there were no differences in this respect between those parents who did and those who did not use any of the services. Thus, the changes described above applied to all parents. Whilst parents who used the services were generally very positive about them, it cannot be shown that they impacted significantly on parent–child relationships. What was interesting though, was that many of those who had *not* used the services, did say that receiving information about the project prompted discussion and dialogue about the project.

Some general learning from these two projects is given below.

Conclusions: learning from the two projects

In the introduction to this chapter, it was proposed that parents of teenagers have fewer sources of information and support available to them compared to the parents of younger children (see Chapter 1 for a discussion). Despite the growth in sources of support during the last few years, there is still very little research-based information available about the effectiveness of providing parents with different forms of help and advice. The authors believe that the school context is a potentially very valuable one for working with parents. It is considered that, as a result of these two pilot studies, a renewed focus should be given to schools as places where parents can receive information and support. The introduction of extended schools by the government also supports the notion that schools have a potentially very broad role to play in family support.

This final section of the chapter identifies the main recommendations arising from the two projects. Although described as recommendations, the majority of the items are not the 'do's and don'ts' of parent support projects, but issues that should be considered and discussed prior to any such projects being set up. All schools are different, parents and young people are different, the aims and objectives of projects will differ, as will the resources available to them. These recommendations are therefore a guide to the lessons that have been learnt in these projects and that need to be considered in the future. The recommendations are divided into three sections, covering: (i) setting up, designing and running parent support projects; (ii) working with parents and young people; and (iii) researching parent support projects.

Setting up, designing and running parent support projects

- *It is essential to canvass the views of parents before a parent support project is established:* This engages parents in the project, and answers any questions that they may have. It also means that the *types* of support parents want can be incorporated into the services that are provided.

- *Consideration must be given to the location of the project:* In the projects described in this chapter, the school location generally worked well, in that it enabled the project to be promoted universally to one group of parents. Locating them in other settings (such as the health service or a community association) would have meant that some parents did not have access to them. Whilst there are some drawbacks to using educational settings (see below), a school context does enable all parents to have access to the services offered.

- *Consideration must be given to the location of the services.* In the projects described in this chapter, it was considered an advantage to have the key players (including the Parent Adviser and the facilitator of the parenting groups) employed from outside the school. It was clear that most parents valued this. However, there were still some parents who had concerns about confidentiality, because of the location of the services in the schools, and the involvement of school staff in the projects. Also, it was clear that some parents were uncomfortable about being visibly seen to participate in the projects, i.e. by attending the courses or consulting the Adviser. The location of such services is an important area for further work.

- *Close liaison must be maintained between all those involved.* It is particularly important that those offering services in these sorts of projects liaise well with each other. In the current projects, for example, the facilitator of the groups recommended that individual parents contact the Parent Adviser, where necessary, for one-to-one support; similarly, the Parent Adviser was able to recommend the use of materials to certain parents. This engaged parents in other parts of the projects, and enabled them to be provided with additional support.

- *Consideration must be given to the age of the young people who are the target of the intervention.* The two projects described in this chapter were aimed either at parents of 12- to 13- or 14- to 15-year-olds. It is of note, however, that few differences were found in either the concerns of parents in these two age groups, or in their use of the services. Thus, for most of the parents in these projects, the need for parenting support was not differentiated by age of the child concerned. This was an unexpected finding and suggests that the need for such support is spread across age groups. It further indicates that such projects should be offered to all parents in a school.

- *The project must be seen as relevant and useful to all parents.* It was clear that for many of the parents, the project was seen as being primarily for those who had difficulties and problems. This is despite the fact that all publicity relating to the projects stressed that all parents might find the services useful. Strategies for ensuring that all parents see projects as useful to them must be developed in the future.

- *Consideration must be given to the impact of gender on projects.* Although these projects found few differences between mothers and fathers on the questionnaire and interview items, gender emerged as an important issue in other areas of the interventions. First, the refusal rate for the interviews was higher amongst the fathers than the mothers in the projects – they indicated that they were either too busy to participate, or did not wish to discuss personal matters with a stranger. Second, the main users of two of the services – the courses and the Parent Adviser - were primarily mothers. Several of the professionals involved in the projects said it was the mothers rather than the fathers who were taking more responsibility for the children in families, including dealing with any problems that arose. Clearly, future work in this area needs to consider – from the outset – that it may be mothers who are using the majority of the services. Strategies to engage fathers must therefore be actively explored.

Working with parents and young people

- *Strategies should be developed to encourage parents to engage in the project.* As stated above, the design of parent support projects must encourage parents to see services as useful and relevant to them. Further, during the course of the project, parents must be further encouraged to use the services. There is no single way of doing this. However, strategies might include: having parents' 'consultation events' throughout the course of the project, to enable parents to ask questions and re-familiarise with a project;

using the views of parents who have already used services to 'sell' the project; and summarising the young people's views, demonstrating their belief in the value of the project.

- *It is important to get young people's views*: Young people can provide valuable information about the relationship between parents and young people. Feedback from young people was gathered in the project at the Adler School. Clearly, more active participation by young people is possible (such as joining in classes with parents) and this also needs to be considered (see also Chapter 10).

- *Accessing information from parents about sensitive issues*: One of the difficulties in these sorts of projects is how to get feedback from parents about their use of the services, when they were dealing with difficult or sensitive issues. For example, parents using the Parent Adviser in these projects were often not sent evaluation forms after they had seen the Adviser; this was because many were facing very difficult issues and some were distressed. It was agreed with the schools that it would be inappropriate to send out evaluation forms at this time. However, other strategies are possible, such as the Parent Adviser completing a form with the parent at the time of the consultation. This needs to be explored in future work.

Researching parent support projects

- It is important to have *personal contact with as many parents as possible* at the beginning of the project, in order to obtain their views and to engage them in considering to use the services.

- The projects raised many issues about *what should be measured* in this type of parent support project. It is not possible to identify a single outcome measure, and to use that as the sole criteria for success of such a project. For example, it was clear that for some parents feeling knowledgeable about adolescent development was a key outcome for them; for others it was to develop new interpersonal skills; for others again it was to feel supported in their parenting. In both projects a wide range of measures was used, relating to knowledge, disagreements, level of support, use of the services and views about the services. These differences in needs between parents have important implications for evaluations that are undertaken.

- It is considered a particularly important recommendation from these projects that *longitudinal data must be collected.* It is often the case that process data only is collected, or that data is collected after the intervention only. Projects assessing the effectiveness of an intervention must collect data before and after. Ideally, follow-up data (perhaps one year on) should also be collected.

Learning for practitioners

- Schools are an important setting for offering information, advice and support to the parents of young people.

- A particular advantage to working with parents in schools is that support can be offered on a universal basis, with more targeted, specialist support offered alongside.

- The development of extended schools is likely to increase the funding and resources aimed at making schools a key resource for parents.

- Parents in both the projects particularly valued having different types of parenting support that they could choose from – i.e. materials for use on their own, interactive sessions and group-based courses, and one-to-one help and advice.

- Whilst having staff external to the school was valued, issues around confidentiality still need to be carefully addressed, to ensure that parents feel confident about using the service.

- Even where parents did not feel in need of any help and advice, they valued having services available should they need them.

8 Using newsletters to support the parents of young people: learning from two studies

Debi Roker and Julie Shepherd

This chapter focuses on an important aspect of support that the Trust for the Study of Adolescence (TSA) has been working on over recent years. This involves the use of *newsletters* as a form of information and support for parents of young people. The TSA has undertaken two projects in this area, one to produce 'general' newsletters for a wide range of parents, and one to produce 'specialist' newsletters for particular groups – e.g. fathers, disabled parents, parents of gay and lesbian children. The chapter highlights the learning from these two projects and includes details of the results of the evaluation into parents' views and experiences of the projects.

There is a growing literature on the parenting of adolescents and the support needs of this group of parents and carers. A key theme emerging from this literature is the fact that parents of adolescents report having insufficient information and support at this time. A number of policy and practice initiatives have emerged in recent years, aimed at providing information, advice and support for this group of parents. Such initiatives include group-based parenting courses, telephone helplines and one-to-one support. However, many of these initiatives are accessed by relatively small numbers of parents and are often expensive to provide.

The TSA was aware that a successful pilot had been undertaken in the US (see Bogenschneider 1997) to provide research-based information and support to parents through the use of newsletters. Providing information in this way was found to be a cost-effective means of reaching large numbers of parents. However, the authors were aware that there had been no proper evaluation of the use of newsletters in the UK. The two projects described in this chapter aimed to evaluate the effectiveness of newsletters as a form of information and support for parents. First, the 'general' newsletter is described.

The 'general newsletters' project

The aims of this project, the development of the newsletters and the main findings are described below.

Aims of the project and development of the newsletters

The aim of this project was to investigate whether general newsletters, aimed at parents of 11- to 16-year-olds, are an effective way of providing information, advice and support to the parents of young people. Specifically, the aim was to explore whether parents read such newsletters, what they think of them and what effect they have on parents' knowledge, views and behaviours. In order to reach a sufficiently large and diverse sample of families to participate in the project, the project was undertaken in collaboration with four schools across England and Wales.

The newsletters were written primarily by TSA staff, following consultation with parents, young people and practitioners. Some articles were written by external contributors. Four newsletters were produced in total, each with a different theme. These were: health; stress and well-being; friends and the peer group; and rules, discipline and communication. Reflecting the discussions with parents and practitioners, the newsletters included:

- information and statistics
- short articles
- an 'agony aunt' page
- a young people's page
- a list of national and local organisations that could provide further information.

The newsletters were designed by a professional designer and comprised eight sides of A4 paper. They were printed on glossy paper and contained photographs of young people and parents. The newsletters were sent directly to parents' homes (see below), approximately one per term.

The four schools involved in the project were primarily located in working-class and disadvantaged communities. One school was included because it had a large proportion of minority ethnic families. Approximately 4000 families across the four schools were involved in the project. Data was collected for the evaluation in a number of different ways:

- *Core family interviews:* 40 'core' families (involving at least one young person and one parent) were interviewed at three time points.

- *Telephone interviews:* Telephone interviews with parents were undertaken after each newsletter was distributed. In total, 802 interviews were conducted, approximately 50 at each school after each of the four newsletters was sent out.

- *Self-completion questionnaires:* A questionnaire was sent to all parents at the end of the project (573 were returned).

Each of the research methods used focused on the following: whether parents read the newsletters; parents' views of the newsletters; and the impact of the newsletters on their knowledge, communication and behaviours. Young people were also asked about their views of the newsletters and the impact they had on their family.

Main results

The main results are summarised below, structured according to the four research questions that were explored in the study:

RESEARCH QUESTION 1: WHICH PARENTS DO AND WHICH DO NOT READ NEWSLETTERS FOR PARENTS OF TEENAGERS? DO YOUNG PEOPLE ALSO READ THEM?

- Approximately half of the parents interviewed by telephone had read each of the newsletters. The lowest figure was 41 per cent of parents who read Newsletter 3 and the highest was 54 per cent who read Newsletter 1.

- Of those interviewed over the telephone, twice as many mothers (60%) as fathers (34%) read the newsletters. However, although less fathers read the newsletters, this still represents one-third of a hard-to-reach group.

- There were very few differences between the four schools in terms of the number of parents reading the newsletters.

- Of those interviewed over the telephone, mothers and fathers reported finding Newsletters 2, 3 and 4 equally useful; mothers reported finding Newsletter 1 as more useful than fathers did.

- Over 80 per cent of the core family young people who were interviewed had seen one or more of the newsletters. One-quarter of these young people had seen all four.

RESEARCH QUESTION 2: WHAT DO PARENTS THINK OF NEWSLETTERS AS A FORM OF INFORMATION AND SUPPORT? WHAT DO YOUNG PEOPLE THINK?

- The majority of the parents, across all the forms of data collected, were positive about the newsletters. The newsletters were seen as particularly useful in raising awareness and reducing isolation. Hearing the perspectives of young people was also valued.

- Most parents believed that the length of the articles, and the length and tone of the newsletters, were 'just about right'.

- Those parents interviewed over the telephone rated each newsletter overall between 3.6 and 3.8, on a five-point scale where five was 'very useful'.

- Those parents who returned the questionnaires at the end of the project were very positive about the project, rating the project as 4.0 overall on the five-point scale.

- Rating the project as a whole, the mean score for the parents was 3.7, suggesting a generally positive view.

- The core family young people were very positive about the project. They rated it 3.8 overall. The young people were particularly positive about the inclusion of the young people's page.

RESEARCH QUESTION 3: WHAT EFFECT DO THE NEWSLETTERS HAVE ON PARENTS' KNOWLEDGE, ATTITUDES AND BEHAVIOURS?

- By the end of the project, fewer of the core family parents reported having worries or concerns about their children and fewer felt that they needed more information about the adolescent years.

- Both the core family and telephone interview parents reported some limited impact on their behaviour as a result of the newsletter project, such as how they communicated with their children and how they behaved as parents.

- The majority of parents across all the data collection forms said that the newsletters provided them with information about where to go for help if they needed it. Most planned to keep the newsletters for future reference.

RESEARCH QUESTION 4: HOW DO THE ABOVE FACTORS VARY BY GENDER, ETHNICITY AND SOCIAL BACKGROUND?

- *Gender:* The results from the telephone interviews showed that more mothers than fathers read the newsletters and were more positive about many aspects. It should be emphasised, however, that one-third of the fathers still read the newsletters.

- *Ethnicity:* The school with a large minority ethnic population had similar proportions of parents reading the newsletters as the other schools. However, only a small number of non-English-speaking parents requested a translated copy of the newsletters, which may indicate that they were not seen as culturally appropriate or of interest.

- *Social background:* The parents at the three schools in predominantly working-class and disadvantaged areas were more positive about the newsletters. They rated the project more highly overall and commented on the fact that the newsletters were easy to read and interesting. The parents at the middle-class school were more likely to comment on the simplistic nature of the newsletters.

Some of the issues raised by this project are addressed later in the chapter. Next, however, TSA's second newsletter project is described.

The 'community newsletters' project
Aims of the project and development of the newsletters

The 'community newsletters' project was designed to develop and extend the 'general newsletters' project described above. The aim was to produce and evaluate 'tailor-made' newsletters for particular groups of parents, such as fathers, lone parents, disabled parents and parents of young people with special needs. There were three specific aims to the community newsletters project:

- to work with a range of community and support groups to design and produce newsletters for particular groups of parents, or parents in particular circumstances

- to evaluate the use of the newsletters by parents and community groups and their effectiveness

- to produce a Good Practice Guide from the project, in order to widely disseminate the learning from it.

The TSA worked with seven community or support groups in order to develop specific newsletters in relation to parenting young people. These groups were:

- Disability, Pregnancy and Parenthood *international* (DPPi) and Disabled Parents Network (DPN) – a support and campaigning network for disabled parents

- Families and Friends of Lesbians and Gays (FFLAG) – a support and campaigning group for parents of lesbian, gay and bisexual children

- Gingerbread South-East – a support group for lone parents

- The Lighthouse Project – a church-based fathers' group

- Southall Contact a Family – a support group for Asian families with a disabled child

- Men United Fathers' Network – a support group for fathers

- The Whole Parents Support Group – a support group (linked to a Youth Offending Team) for parents of young people with special needs and/or at risk of offending.

Each of the seven newsletters was developed in collaboration with parents and workers at the groups. The newsletters contained parents' stories, 'hints and tips', expert views and information and resources. The newsletters were all in colour, 8 to 12 pages long and in 'magazine' style. At the end of the project all groups were given the newsletter template, in order to produce further editions.

An evaluation of the process and outcomes of the community newsletters project was also undertaken. This involved interviews with workers at each group before and after newsletter production. Also, parents were either interviewed or completed a self-completion question-naire, in relation to their views about the newsletters, and whether it affected their knowledge or behaviour – 70 parents provided data for the evaluation.

Main results

The main results of the community newsletters project are given below, focusing on general views and use of the newsletters, the views of project workers and the impact on the groups, and the future of the newsletters at the groups.

GENERAL VIEWS AND USE OF THE NEWSLETTERS

In general, the parents and workers at each of the seven groups were very positive about the newsletters. In all seven community groups, a large majority of parents reported that the newsletters had (a) been read by others in the household, (b) had prompted discussion about parenting issues, and (c) had had a positive effect on their knowledge and parent–child relationships. Some quotations from the parents demon-strate what they liked about the newsletter. First, people liked the layout and content:

> The parent story – it's good to hear positive experiences – that has to be tempered with the real-life difficulties and stress of parenting when you/parents feel ashamed or embarrassed of their disability.

The layout is nice, clear print on good colour-contrasting background, whilst adding different colours that help identify articles and is visually interesting.

I particularly liked the parent and children's stories.

The book list and the websites I found most useful.

It [the newsletter] was very supportive and easy to read.

As a parent of a gay son, any information is helpful, especially when your child first comes out. It is no longer an issue for our family but I found the newsletter interesting and helpful.

Second, parents described how they found the newsletter supportive:

Being reminded that there are lots of other parents in the same/ similar situation to us.

The sharing of experiences with others makes one feel that they're not alone with their feelings and worries and that is reassuring.

I think the newsletter is a marvellous idea. It will help parents understand more about issues. A lot of children are in turmoil and suicidal. I think the newsletter can only do good.

I feel a newsletter is vital for parents because it really helps to read other people's stories. I was 'cool' when my daughter told me but no matter how 'cool' you are it takes some adjusting to your child being gay.

Finally, many parents talked about how their children and young people read the newsletter, and found it useful:

They found it really useful – three other friends saw it and my teenage son.

The newsletter was very good. My daughter read bits of it and really liked it.

I think the project is a good idea. Although my son is not a teenager now the issues are still real and I look forward to receiving future issues.

It was a great source of comfort.

As these comments show, parents were extremely positive about the newsletter.

VIEWS OF PROJECT WORKERS AND THE IMPACT ON THE GROUPS

Workers in all seven organisations commented on the value of the newsletters, in two main ways. First, they considered that the newsletters provided targeted information and support to the parents that they worked with, i.e. with particular needs, such as disability or lone parenting. Further evidence of the value of the newsletters is contained in the figures for those who used the 'further information' sections. Almost one-third of the parents (30%) said that they had contacted an organisation listed in the newsletter or looked at one of the websites. This was in contrast to TSA's 'general newsletters' project (above), where less than 5 per cent of the parents had contacted organisations or websites listed on the back page. It may be that when information is tailored to the specific needs of parents, it is more likely to be drawn upon for information and support. This is a significant advantage of a targeted newsletter approach.

Second, the workers commented that developing the newsletters had enabled the parents they work with to raise and discuss issues – in each case the development of the newsletter was seen as a valuable 'community development' activity for the parents and the group. For example:

> The sense of a joint effort, by all concerned, to produce the final results.

> They feel really proud to have contributed. It gave them the chance to be heard and voice the issues that they face.

> Getting the Punjabi version and having a newsletter discussing the issues and problems that our families face.

As is described below, most parents and workers hoped that the newsletters would continue.

FUTURE OF THE NEWSLETTERS AT THE GROUPS

The majority of parents (89%) thought that the group to which they belonged should produce its own newsletter in the future. This added further weight to the parents' positive views about the newsletters. There was less agreement about how often the newsletters should be produced, with parents' views ranging from once a month, to once a year. Most of the groups planned to use the newsletters in a broad range of ways in the future – to recruit and support new members, to raise awareness of issues for their parents and to fundraise. Some also planned to produce their own newsletters in the future. Two examples from the fathers' project demonstrate this well:

> I thought it was very positive in what it was trying to achieve. Good source of contact for other dads. Good to see something aimed at dads. I would be disappointed if it did not continue!

> Excellent. It is important to continue with it and to use it as a link point between fathers in the area; to initiate different types of groups and to provide a contact point for people to get information and support on the issues that are covered that directly affect them.

All of the project workers said that they would continue to use the newsletter in some way. Some planned to distribute it to a wider range of parents, in order to provide information and support to other parents. In addition to this the groups said that they planned to use the newsletter to raise awareness of the issues facing their parents, to fundraise, to promote their work and to attract new members. Thus, whilst the newsletter was clearly a valued resource for individual parents, it was also a resource for groups to use in order to develop and extend their work.

At the end of the project, all the groups were given a copy of their newsletter template as a Microsoft Word document. This was done in order to make it easy for them to produce more copies of the first newsletter, or to develop more editions in the future. The majority of the workers interviewed said that they felt their group *would* produce more newsletters in the future. This is a very positive finding in terms of encouraging and supporting sustainability. The workers were also very positive about the Good Practice Guide that was produced in this project, and felt that this provided valuable learning for the future for themselves and other groups.

Themes and issues arising in both projects

The two projects described in this chapter – the 'general' and 'community' newsletters projects – aimed to explore a key question in parenting support. Are newsletters (both general and specialist/targeted) effective as a form of information, advice and support for parents of young people? This final section of the chapter explores this further. A number of learning points emerge from the newsletters projects:

- *Using newsletters to support parents:* These projects have shown that newsletters *are* an effective way of providing information and support to parents in general, as well as parents of teenagers with particular needs, or living in particular circumstances. The parents involved in the projects found that the newsletters had a positive benefit, in terms of sharing experiences, reducing isolation and contributing to enhanced communication with their children. Parents also used them to get more specialist help and support from other organisations.

- *Strategies for distributing the newsletters:* In the general newsletter project, the newsletters were distributed directly to people's homes. However, there was evidence that in two-parent households fathers often did not get to see the newsletters. Other ways of distributing newsletters might be needed in order to make them more widely available. This could include general practitioner surgeries, chemists, job centres and supermarkets.

- *Cost-effectiveness of newsletters:* The newsletters cost approximately 50 pence each to design and print. This is relatively inexpensive, compared to other forms of help and support. It was interesting to find that many of the practitioners involved in the projects were surprised that the newsletters were this cheap to produce. In addition, many planned to produce their own newsletters in future (by printing them in-house), thus reducing the overall cost.

- *Addressing literacy issues:* The use of newsletters is clearly dependent on the literacy skills of parents. It was unclear from the projects how many parents did not have access to the newsletters because of literacy issues. This could be addressed, however, by making the newsletters available in more accessible formats. This has now been undertaken by TSA (see later), which has produced the general newsletters both on audiotape and in large print.

- *Groups most suited to specialist newsletters.* The community newsletters project showed that the groups most suited to getting involved in newsletter development were those that were quite established, with a committed group of members. Many of the groups in this project were in fact affiliated to larger organisations such as Gingerbread and Contact a Family; other groups were part of a local Youth Offending Team. This structure and ongoing support meant that it was easier for them to commit the time and effort needed to create a newsletter. Other less structured or insecure community groups may find this more of a challenge. In addition, established groups are more likely to be able to secure financial support to enable them to produce a newsletter.

- *The amount of time needed to develop newsletters.* It should be stressed that all the newsletters took much more time to plan and prepare than had been anticipated. Thus, getting parents' views about content, receiving parents' articles and ideas and getting views on the first draft were very time-consuming. It is essential that groups understand the time and commitment involved, if they decide to produce a newsletter for the parents who they work with. A parenting support or community group is likely to be disappointed if a newsletter project, once underway, ends prematurely.

- *Meeting diverse needs.* There was limited use in the community newsletter project of the translation services made available for those parents speaking different languages. More work needs to be done to address the needs of minority ethnic groups, particularly those with English as a second language (again, see later). It may be, of course, that the newsletters were not appropriate to those in different cultural groups. Further research is needed into this.

- *Reaching fathers.* Although less fathers than mothers read the newsletters, a significant proportion of fathers were still reached by the project. Newsletters could therefore be a valuable way of reaching fathers of teenagers. However, different strategies may need to be tried out to reach more fathers, such as those described above.

- *Distributing the learning from this project.* There was a considerable amount of learning from the two projects. The learning from the community newsletters project has been summarised in a Good Practice Guide, which is available from TSA.

- *Dealing with difficult issues.* In any project involving a diverse group of parents and practitioners, it is inevitable that difficult and contentious issues will arise. There were many such issues in the project. Some differences of opinion arose between groups (both between parents, and between parents and workers), with other issues arising between groups and TSA staff. The issues that arose generally related to decision making, and the authority to decide on such things as revising deadlines, content of the newsletters (including photographs) and issues to leave out because of insufficient space.

The issues that arose were all resolved in one way or another, and none of the newsletters that were produced failed to be circulated because of the issues that arose within the group. It is useful to highlight and review the sorts of issues that came up in the projects. Some of the issues were quite sensitive for projects, and groups could be easily identified if they were described in detail here. They are therefore presented in an anonymised way here. They are described in the Good Practice Guide that has been produced from the projects as issues for groups to talk about, in order to anticipate the sorts of issues that arise in preparing newsletters for parents. These examples are reproduced here, in order to illustrate the sorts of issues that came up:

- A parent said she would write an article for your newsletter. The deadline you agreed was over two weeks ago, but still she hasn't done it. She keeps saying she'll get it to you 'soon', and that she really wants to have her article in the newsletter. *What do you do?*

- A couple write an article for the newsletter, on how they coped with their son's drug abuse. They want to use their real names, and their son's real name, in the article. However, all the other parents' stories in the newsletter are anonymous. *What do you do?*

- You are part of a parents' support group, which is connected to a national charity. The newsletter your group has produced has a lot of quotes from young people and parents in it. Quite a few of these quotes contain swear words. The parents think this is fine. However, the national charity says that if the swear words are not taken out, the charity will withdraw its financial support for the group. *What do you do?*

- You are a parent who has been the main volunteer on your group's newsletter. The newsletter is now finished and ready to be printed. Then someone asks whether you have permission to include extracts from a recently published book. You realise you had not thought about copyright issues. *What do you do?*

- Your charity has been working with a group of parents to produce a newsletter, aimed at single parents. The newsletter includes a photograph of one local branch, where the parents were having a night out. Some of the parents have now seen the photograph and do not want it included, as they look 'the worse for wear'. Other parents really like it, as it focuses on the group having fun. *What do you do?*

In one form or another, all of these issues arose in the 'community newsletters' project. It is therefore important that organisations working to produce newsletters in the future, consider and address these issues at the start.

In conclusion, the authors believe that both the projects described in this chapter point to one conclusion. This is that newsletters have a great deal to offer the field of parenting support.

Learning for practitioners

- Newsletters have the potential to be a well-used and well-received form of support for the parents of young people.

- Parents are very positive about newsletters. They find the information informative and useful, and they find the newsletters reassuring. They also like hearing other parents' perspectives and stories.

- Newsletters can be produced that are general in nature (i.e. that can be used by all parents) or are in more specialist or targeted formats (i.e. for parents in particular circumstances or with par- ticular needs).

- Newsletters can be produced inexpensively, at around 50 pence per copy for professionally produced versions. Costs are much cheaper if newsletters are produced 'in-house'.

- Issues of literacy need to be addressed when using newsletters. Producing newsletters in large print and on audiotape can help to address these issues.

- When producing newsletters with parents or community groups, potentially difficult issues (such as editorial control or anonymity of articles) need to be discussed and agreed in advance.

References

Bogenschneider, K. and Stone, M. (1997) 'Delievering parent education to low and high risk parents of adolescents via age-paced newsletters.' *Family Relations 46*, 2, 123–134.

9 Getting information and support from websites

Debi Roker

This chapter describes research undertaken at the Trust for the Study of Adolescence (TSA), which looked at how parents use websites to get information and support. There is now an increasing use of websites as a way of getting information and support to people, including parents and carers. In recent years there has been a rapid increase in the number of organisations that have a website, in order to get information about their activities, and information and advice, to parents and others. There are now few organisations – either in the statutory or the voluntary sector – that do not have a website. Indeed, anecdotal evidence suggests that websites have become a key feature of any organisation's work.

More and more families now have access to the internet at home and/or at work. A recent survey by the British Computer Society (BCS 2004) for example showed that three-quarters of the UK population have used a computer, either infrequently or regularly. As this also shows, however, a quarter of the population have never used computers, and this figure increases amongst older populations. Other research confirms that those with the most limited access or use are amongst the most disadvantaged groups (Loader and Keeble 2004).

There is surprisingly little research-based information about how parents use the internet to get information and advice. A relatively small-scale study undertaken several years ago (Griffey 2001) showed how positive many parents were about getting information and support via websites. However, this study focused primarily on parents of younger children – less is known about the needs of parents of teenagers in relation to websites. Where research has been done in relation to parents and websites, it has mainly been in relation to health advice and information (for example, Eysenbach and Kohler 2002; Williams *et al.* 2002).

There has been little opportunity to investigate current provision, including how organisations plan and structure the information and support they provide to parents via websites. In addition, there has been no real investigation of *parents'* views and experiences in this respect and whether websites are actually meeting the needs of parents. Further, there is little information about good practice, which existing organisations can use to improve their websites, or that new organisations can use when creating their websites. If this form of support is to develop and grow, then it is important to monitor standards in website provision and to ensure that they are meeting parents' needs.

The project described in this chapter was funded by a grant from the Parenting Fund, administered by the Department for Education and Skills (DfES). It was undertaken between January and December 2004. The aim of the study was to undertake research with parents, to identify (i) their general views about getting information and support via websites, and (ii) their views about the style, format, content, etc. of different websites.

The research

A total of 71 parents took part in the research, which was undertaken in different locations across England. The sample was diverse in terms of gender, family type, social background and ethnicity.

There were two parts to the research. The first part involved a general discussion with parents about their use of information technology in general, and the internet in particular. This then moved on to their views about using the internet to get information and advice, and then specifically in relation to getting advice about parenting. Parents were also asked if they had ever sought information or advice via the internet, and if so, what about, and how useful this was. This was designed both as an introduction to the project and to the issues, and to gather data on previous history of using websites in relation to parenting issues.

The main part of the research had two elements and was undertaken with parents sitting in front of computer terminals. First, parents were given four scenarios to work through, relating to 'typical' issues for parents (for example, about alcohol use, effects of divorce, etc.). These are detailed in full in the section 'Views about websites using the four scenarios'.

After reading out each scenario, parents were asked to identify websites that they thought could help provide information and advice on these issues. Once websites were identified, parents were asked to comment on a range of factors about these sites – these included the ease of navigation of the website, its appearance, language used, style, format, presentation of parenting advice and information, etc.

The main results from the research are described below, as follows:

- use of the internet in general, and in relation to getting parenting support

- views about websites using the four scenarios

- parents' likes and dislikes about website design, style and content.

Use of the internet in general, and in relation to getting parenting support

At the start of the individual and group sessions, parents' general views about computers and the internet were explored, as well as their experiences of getting parenting information and support from the internet. These two areas are explored separately below.

Use of the internet in general

There was a very wide range of experience in relation to experience of information technology (IT), computers and the internet. No formalised assessment was made of this, but parents were grouped according to their level of experience. A small number of parents (approximately 8 to 10 of the 71) were very experienced in this respect, using computers (including the internet) in their work and home lives. They were familiar with internet searching and the different layouts of websites. For example:

> Yeah I, well we, use it all the time, sometimes too much [laughs]. At work, with the kids, for my banking, booking holidays, that sort of thing. I'm a real convert.

A majority of the parents (46) had some, limited, knowledge of computers and the internet. These parents had often used computers and the internet in limited settings, either on training courses, or at work. They had occasionally looked up specific pieces of information on the internet. For example:

> Yes I know the general principles, I can work my way around.

This group did not consider themselves terribly experienced in this respect, and some were slightly anxious at the start of the research:

> …I sort of know the basics, what does what, but just in a really basic way. I might need to help today to find some of these websites to look at [laughs].

Many of this group had also had mixed experiences of using the internet. For example, some were positive:

> …there's a huge amount on there, a lot of good information and stuff, but you have to work at it…it's worth it though, it really is…

Others were less positive:

> …sometimes I just give up, with the ads [advertisements] popping up all the time, I don't know how to stop them, and then sometimes I just get lost and give up.

The final group of parents (14) described themselves as never having used computers or the internet, or having very limited experience of doing so. Some of these parents did not have access to a computer and did not know how they would go about using one. It is of note that many of the black and minority ethnic (BME) parents in the study fell into this category – one of the fieldworkers who undertook the research with this group commented that: 'Black parents are only now starting to get to grips with computers and the internet'. Other parents had literacy difficulties that made using a computer problematic. As this parent explained it:

> Nope…I've not done any computer things, it always looks too difficult, but my youngest says it's not. I'll give it a go…

This latter group of parents undertook the research either in a group with more experienced internet users, or with help from the fieldworkers.

Use of the internet to get parenting information and support

The parents were then asked about their experiences of getting information and support via the internet in relation to *parenting*. There were mixed responses to this. The majority of those who regularly or occasionally used the internet (the 60 or so parents referred to above), had *not* tried to get any information about parenting from the internet. This was mainly because parents had not needed any information or support – as this parent explained it:

> I've never wanted anything about being a parent or about my kids, so I haven't needed to...

> No I haven't looked up issues on the internet...because I still believe that parents talk to each other, especially when you are in a group of parents and all the children are the same age, normally the children are facing the same sort of thing at the same time really...I would feel quite lonely if I had to go on the internet really.

Some parents also felt that the internet was not appropriate for them, as they would prefer to talk things through with someone if they had a problem:

> I don't think I'd use the internet as a parent, no. I'd like to talk to people, you know, on the phone.

Some also felt that if you had a problem the internet might not be the best place to get help:

> [I'd] need something more direct, give more information about the actual subject we're looking for. If you're distraught the last thing you will want to do is to go looking all over the place, [you] need something more instant to look at.

It is of note, in this respect, that most of the BME parents in the study were sceptical about getting information and support via the internet. Many of the BME parents commented that problems or issues within the family should be dealt with within the family, the extended family, or with friends. The internet was rarely used for this. One Pakistani father, for example, said that he would never use the internet for advice about his children:

> You don't go to outside agencies to get help, and I certainly wouldn't use the internet for it.

Another Indian parent made a similar comment:

> No, I don't think many Asian parents would think to use the internet. They would speak to their parents, like I would, or sisters. No I wouldn't go to the internet for anything about my role as a parent.

It is of note, however, that a few black and Asian parents thought the opposite – i.e. that the internet was a useful source of advice because it was anonymous, and did not require talking to others in the community. Some of the BME parents described the internet as a source of reassurance for them, as well as being secure and confidential. For example:

> It's nice to know that other parents have the same problem. Being Asian you think you're unique, like you're the only person with difficulties, you think besti besti [shame, shame].

Other parents also said that they had not ever thought about using the internet in this way, i.e. as a way of getting information and advice about parenting. For many this was the first time they had thought of the internet in this way:

> ...that's interesting that, I just would never have thought... going to websites and getting advice. No, to be honest it just never occurred to me...

> No, well, not about being a parent. Is there stuff on the internet about that?

This latter point was one that came up quite often – many parents had thought about the internet as being available to provide factual information, such as getting details for organisations, shopping, or looking up a particular illness. Most did not think of it as a source of general information and advice in relation to bringing up children. As this father explained it:

> It wouldn't occur to me to look for anything like that on the internet, I wouldn't have thought there was anything on there like that.

As will also be mentioned later in this section, many of the parents added that they would not know where to start to get information in this way:

> When I go on the internet I just think, sometimes, where do you start? You know there's just so much.

> That's why I'm here in a way [laughs]. I'm hoping I'll learn what's where, and how to get at information.

A small number of parents in the study, however, *had* used the internet in the past in order to get information, advice or support in relation to parenting issues. This generally involved those parents who felt most confident about the internet and who used it on a daily basis. These parents had looked up a range of topics, including the following:

- special needs diagnoses and related issues, mainly in relation to Attention Deficit Hyperactivity Disorder (ADHD) and dyslexia

- how to make appeals in school exclusions

- information about the changes of puberty and when these usually start

- what 'parent contracts' in schools are

- what different types of drugs young people use, and what the signs of drug use are.

The experiences of these parents were generally positive, in that the internet had provided answers to these questions. For example:

> ...yeah really good, just great actually, it gave me exactly what I was looking for...

> ...it's all so up to date, all the latest medical stuff about it [ADHD]. I went back to my GP [general practitioner] about a new treatment the next day.

These parents often described themselves as internet 'converts'. They believed that the internet had enormous potential for helping them to get information and advice in relation to their parenting. The advantages that this group saw the internet as having included the following:

- They are usually very up to date.

- Parents can 'browse around', and look at different views and ideas.

- Parents can use the internet at a time convenient to them.

- Viewing of websites can be done at work or in another setting, away from children if necessary – i.e. more confidential than a telephone call.

Many of these parents believed that more parents would use the internet for parenting advice if they knew how useful and accessible it was. As one recent 'convert' described it:

> I think it's the future, it's up to date, you can get at it easily when you want to. Websites are a really good way to get information and help about your kids.

> It's a waste really, I mean there's just so much here. Doing this today has opened my eyes. People really should be told that there's so much on the internet for parents. I'd never have known if I'd not done this research.

Views about websites using the four scenarios

This section presents the results for the four scenarios that parents were given and the views that parents had about the internet sites that they found. However, an important finding was made early on in the field-work. This was that most parents found searching the internet very difficult. This issue is therefore explored first, followed by the parents' responses to the four scenarios.

Parents' experiences of searching the internet

In tackling the four scenarios (below) it was clear that the majority of parents found it very difficult to start a search and found it hard to get the information they wanted. A number of questions were also raised in the searches, which they did not always know the answer to. The main things that occurred were as follows:

NOT KNOWING HOW TO USE A SEARCH ENGINE

Some of the parents (even those who said they had undertaken internet searches before) were not sure how to undertake a search using a search engine. Some also did not know that there were different search engines available, e.g. Google, Ask Jeeves. Where this happened the interviewer helped at this stage.

USING VERY GENERAL TERMS IN INTERNET SEARCHES

Many of the parents used very general terms when they were searching, such as 'young people and sex' or 'adolescents'. This often led to a very long list of websites coming up, many of which had little connection to the topic they were searching for. As this father said:

> …this is what I mean…trawling through things, this really puts me off because nine times out of ten you'll go through it and it really isn't what you want anyway, it's just a word in the sentence.

Crucially, these general terms often led to websites that were pornographic, which many parents found distressing. Some were also concerned that this could cause problems, if it was thought that they were accessing pornography at home. Some parents said, at that time, that getting to inappropriate websites put them off using the internet.

SPELLING OF KEY TERMS

Linked to the points above, some parents found it difficult to spell some of the key words that they wanted, and so used others. Several parents, for example, found typing the word 'alcohol' difficult and so would put in the word 'drinking' or 'beer'. This often distorted the search and meant that they got an even less appropriate range of websites listed.

SEARCHING WORLDWIDE AS OPPOSED TO UK

Many of the parents were not aware that on most search engines, they could search for UK websites only. Thus, the general terms above (and even the more specific ones) came up with sites from all over the world – the US, Scandinavia and Australia were most common. Many parents did not notice this until they were part way through the website, and then often felt that the information was not relevant because it had to do with another country or culture. Many were frustrated, for example, to find a telephone helpline advertised, and then find it was American.

ORGANISATIONS WITH THE SAME NAME WORLDWIDE

Linked to the issue above, was the fact that many organisations across the world have the same internet address, or are branches of the same body. Thus, for example, Alcoholics Anonymous (AA) has websites in many countries. Often parents did not know that they were in the AA site for New Zealand or Canada. They often only found this out when particular locations were mentioned, or some aspect of the law that was different to the UK. Many parents found this very frustrating.

SPONSORED SITES ON SEARCH ENGINES

When parents undertook a search, many resulted in 'sponsored sites' being listed at the top of the search. Many parents said that they did not know what this meant. Some thought it might be that organisations have paid to be listed on there, others that visitors would have to pay to enter those sites. Many felt anxious about these and as a result did not use them.

REQUIREMENT TO REGISTER IN ORDER TO ACCESS A WEBSITE

Finally, some of the sites that parents chose from their search required parents to register with them before they could access the website. Most parents were either frustrated by this (because of the time it took) or were worried by it (feeling that their details would be used in some way, for example they would be sent junk mail). Most therefore left these sites without registering.

Views about websites based on the four scenarios

In the research project parents went through a number of scenarios (up to four) in order to look at websites and indicate what they thought of them. The results of these searches are given below, with the scenario listed first.

Scenario 1: What would you do?

> You have a 16-year-old son. He's out a lot with friends, and you think he's drinking a lot of alcohol. He has a hangover most mornings, but he says that's 'normal' for people his age.

> You decide to get some information about young people and
> alcohol from the web. Which websites do you go to, and how
> useful are they?

Most parents interpreted this as a scenario about alcohol, and most
started their searches here. Parents generally entered into the search
engines, terms such as 'young people and alcohol', 'alcohol abuse' and
'youth drinking'. Many of the parents found this stage quite difficult:

> Hmm, we want facts, information about alcohol, don't we?
> That's a fact really isn't it, not advice, there's nothing specific I
> can think to search for for that.

> Let's try something general, like 'alcohol' and 'young people'.

As stated above, this generally led to a very long list of websites. Significantly, many of the references on the first page of the search turned out to
be research reports and government policy reports, from different countries across the world. This was not always evident, however, when
parents first saw the website listed, and this often led to frustration:

> This is like I said earlier...you think 'yep that's it, that will have
> it' and then it's something completely different, not what you
> want at all.

Some parents also found that they entered websites, followed the links
suggested, but often this resulted in a circular process. As this father
explained, his search started at the BBC Health website, and after following several links found he was back there again:

> Look – after all that we're back to the start, which is annoying.
> If it was 2 o'clock in the morning I'd certainly have given up by
> now. It can just feel such a waste of time.

A wide range of websites came up in these searches, including:

> www.questia.com
>
> www.bupa.co.uk
>
> www.alcoholconcern.org.uk
>
> www.happiness.com
>
> www.lamplight.com

www.focusas.com

www.child.net

www.channel4.co.uk/health

Most of these were not considered appropriate when parents entered them. In particular, some of the recommended websites – such as the UK Department of Health (www.dh.gov.uk) – were very large websites that took a considerable time to download. Parents found this frustrating and often abandoned trying to access the information there.

Following this early searching, most of the parents then focused in on names that they recognised – the most common one was the site for Alcoholics Anonymous (AA). As this organisation was familiar to most of the parents, it meant it was trusted by many of them:

> I would look at this, yes. They're a good organisation, I've heard of them, I would trust what they say…

As mentioned above, however, parents often found themselves on the American or Australian AA site, without always being aware of this. This was frustrating if parents said they would consider approaching a local self-help group. However, these sites often did provide useful information, particularly around the issue of what 'problem' drinking is.

Several of the groups of parents also thought about looking at the Connexions website (www.connexions.gov.uk), or the Talk To Frank website (www.talktofrank.com), in relation to this scenario. Two queries were raised about this, however. First, parents were not sure whether Talk To Frank was for young people only, or whether parents could use it too. Second, they were not sure whether either of the organisations concerned would deal only with illegal drugs, and not with alcohol.

Scenario 2: What would you do?

> You are the parent of a 12-year-old girl. She's just started at secondary school and you're worried that she's not settling in. She seems to have made no new friends and finds the amount of homework difficult. Now, most mornings, she's saying that she doesn't want to go to school. She also says she doesn't want to talk to you about it. You decide to try and get some help and

advice via websites. Which websites do you get to, and how useful are they?

This scenario was interpreted in a number of different ways by the parents. Some parents considered that this issue was mainly about the transition to secondary school, not about settling in; others thought it was about parent–child relationships and communication. Many also considered that the child was probably being bullied and that the internet search should therefore concentrate on that.

There was thus a variety of internet searches undertaken by the parents. Parents generally entered the following terms into the search engines:

- 'children and bullying'
- 'settling in to secondary school'
- 'withdrawn children'
- 'problems at school'
- 'children making friends'.

Again this resulted in a very large number of internet addresses coming up in the search. As in Scenario 1, many of the results listed turned out to be research reports or policy documents. Several of these searches led to parents reaching www.bullying.co.uk, which was considered to be an excellent site – practical, reassuring and full of useful information about what to do. A large number of US and Australian sites also came up on the searches, which were generally considered to be less appropriate or useful. Several of the parents also searched for the websites of Kidscape (www.kidscape.org.uk) and Childline (www.childline.org.uk), which they thought might be useful for the daughter to look at.

Two additional findings were of note in relation to this scenario. First, many of the searches undertaken resulted in parents being referred to the BBC website – www.bbc.co.uk/parenting. Many were immediately attracted to this website, both because of its layout and design (clear, good-sized print, easy to navigate), but also because it was 'trusted'. As these parents explained it:

It's a bright site and the thing about the BBC is that you would trust it and…it has been written and researched by people who are able to make it clear…I think the BBC is a very good starting point for people who don't know where to go.

You do always look for something that makes it legitimate…you think 'Oh good, I can trust that'…you are looking for authority, and the BBC does that…

I'd certainly go to this one yeah [the BBC]. I, kind of, well I trust them you know, that they're on the ball, that they're honest kind of thing. This would be a really good place to start with any of those other problems that we've just done.

The second interesting finding that came up under this scenario, was that many of the parents said that they would go to the *school's* website. This was for two reasons. First, parents felt that '…the school's bullying policy will be on there', along with other policies that might be helpful. Second, they felt that the website would explain who parents can contact about personal or pastoral issues. In general, many parents felt that it would give them a place to start, in looking for information. Thus, a large number of parents tried to access the website for their child's school. This often proved difficult – some were under construction, some were not available and others did not have policies (such as their bullying policy) on the website. Some parents also thought that there would be links on schools' websites, to useful sources of help and support for parents – however, this was often not the case. As this mother stated:

Well I'd just put that BBC Parenting link on there, that's got everything really. Every school should have that on, so if you're having problems you know where to go.

Scenario 3: What would you do?

You are the father of young people aged 11, 14 and 15. You and your wife have decided to get divorced. Before you tell your children, you decide to get more information and advice about helping them to deal with this. Which websites do you go to, and how helpful are they?

This scenario, like Scenario 2, raised a number of different issues for parents. Some saw it as an issue for the couple, whilst others saw it as an issue specifically for the father. This therefore led to a number of different search strategies in the fieldwork. The terms entered in the search engines included the following:

- 'children and divorce'
- 'fathers getting divorced'
- 'supporting children'
- 'family breakdown, getting help'
- 'couples with children splitting up'.

These searches often led to a very long list of websites, from all over the world. Many of the websites that were listed were legal ones, including legal reports and judgments in legal issues. Many of the parents found this very frustrating. Where parents decided to start again (as many did), they went to specific websites. Those chosen were mainly the websites for Families Need Fathers, and Relate – both were considered to have some useful information in them in relation to this topic. One additional website was mentioned in several locations – www.divorce.co.uk – which had some useful information on it. However, the parents were sometimes suspicious of this site because it was not clear who had set it up. A link was also found to the American site www.equalparenting.org, which many parents found useful.

Overall, many of the parents commented on how difficult it was to get information on this issue. As one parent explained it:

> ...you would think that there'd be more, it's such a common thing, people splitting up. I'm amazed there's not more on this, you know, guidance about talking to children about it.

> It's probably on there, but, well, where do you start? I think we're shooting in the dark.

Many of the parents in the sessions concluded that addressing this scenario had taken the greatest amount of time, but that they had got the least from it. Many suggested that if they had been at home, on their own, they would have given up. Some added that this sort of problem was better dealt with by going to the local library or Citizen's Advice Bureau.

Scenario 4: What would you do?

> You are the single parent of young people aged 12 and 15. You're feeling increasingly drained by your relationship with them. They argue with you about everything and are often rude and abusive. There's a constant air of tension in the home. You feel at the end of your tether. You decide to see what information or support there is on the web, to help you cope. What do you find, and how useful is it?

In trying to find information on the internet about this issue, the parents had different views as to what it was about and where the search should go. The following phrases were used in the searches:

- 'rude children'
- 'teenage years'
- 'single parents and children'
- 'coping with teenagers'
- 'dealing with aggressive teenagers'.

As before, these searches led to a long list of websites, most of which the parents had never heard of. As they looked at different ones, it was clear that some were American, Canadian and Australian sites. These included websites such as www.sarahnewton.com, and www.parentingcenter.com. Many of these used language and terms that the parents were not familiar with or did not like and which contained pictures of 'smiling well-dressed teenagers', as one parent put it. As in the previous scenario, many parents thought their child's school website might have useful information:

> You would think there'd be stuff on there, about coping with kids. It really should be on there. I bet that's where most parents would try first.

> ...I'm sure there'd be information about this on the school's website, or like links to places that can help.

A lot of the searches above also resulted in parents reaching special needs and mental health websites, addressing issues such as violence, aggression and offending. This was not what most parents wanted:

> ...that's the problem – we want general information, not spe-
> cialist, you know, problem kids stuff.

Again these were considered to be unhelpful in addressing the issue concerned. Many of the parents added that this issue was too difficult to
address via a website. As this father explained:

> If I had this problem I would never look on a website. It's too
> complicated to look up. You can't just pick out words and get
> the right answer. I think you'd have to speak to a friend, or call a
> helpline or something.

Parents' likes and dislikes about website design, style and content

Some consistent patterns emerged in the research, about what parents
liked and disliked about different websites, and what they found helpful
and not helpful in getting advice about parenting. These aspects are summarised below.

What parents did *not* like on websites

There were a number of things that parents did *not* like, or that put them
off using the information contained in a website. These were as follows:

- A website having old or out-of-date information on it and/or
  not having a date on it to say when it was last updated – this
  was particularly important for parents looking for information
  about drugs or medical treatments:

  > ...that was so frustrating, seeing that it hasn't been updated for
  > years...what a waste of time.

- Websites where part or all of the website is 'under construction'
  – as one parent explained:

  > ...it says to come back later, but really, are you likely to? It's
  > now or never really...

- Very large websites with no clear system for showing visitors
  how the website is structured:

  > ...as you saw, we just had to give up on some, they were too
  > difficult.

- Websites that had an internal search engine, but nothing came up when 'black parents' or 'BME parents' was entered. This was particularly disappointing where parents felt the graphics or front page was 'encouraging' to BME parents. Many BME parents found it very frustrating when there was nothing specific at the end of a search:

   ...that, yes, that made me feel, like, I should go in there, as a black man I mean, a black dad.

- Websites that did not have a button or menu on the front page which said 'Information for parents'. Without this, many parents felt that there was no 'invitation' to them to enter the site, or that the site might only include information for practitioners:

   You have to feel like they're saying 'come on in', if you know what I mean [laughs] ...no really I mean you sort, like you know it's for people like you, for parents.

- Websites with obscure or general titles, which have no information about who the website was set up by, or who runs it:

   I'm immediately suspicious, like that one where we couldn't see who it was run by. You wouldn't talk to someone on the phone and not know who they are.

- Websites with very 'busy' home pages, with lots of information on – this was considered very off-putting:

   Oh god that was just too much. I don't find reading easy anyway, and that was just too much.

- Websites that had very small writing:

   ...it's an immediate turn off, literally.

- Websites with flashing graphics and animations:

   I'm sure the person who invented this one enjoyed doing it but all those symbols and photos jumping about – it gave me a headache.

- Websites that contained advertising, in particular pop-ups:

  > No, that's not on, that shouldn't be on there. I wouldn't stay in this one because it's got advertising on. I'm not here to buy stuff.

- Home pages that have 'FAQs' at the top – many parents did not know what this meant, and found it off-putting to have this on a front page:

  > ...not sure about other people but you feel awkward, you know, if you don't understand something...it feels likes it's all, you know, whoosh, over my head.

- Having to register before you can enter the site – this occurred many times during the fieldwork:

  > ...that was really irritating, we just wanted to have a look, and once they get your email address who knows what they'll do with it.

- Sections of websites that state 'download here', without giving any reassurance about whether they are protected from viruses:

  > ...you hear it all the time, don't download things from the internet, so no I wouldn't.

- Websites that only have information for parents that they have to buy:

  > ...you feel you're in a shop, you know, rather than a charity or whatever – it's buy this and buy that...some stuff should be free.

What parents *did* like on websites

There were also many aspects that parents *did* like about the websites that they entered and that made them feel positive about the site. Crucially, these aspects were more likely to make people trust the site, value what it said and follow the links that it suggested. Some, not surprisingly, are the opposite of the things above and some are new things. The things that parents liked included the following:

- A clear home page, saying who the organisation is, what they do and how the website is structured:

  If it's not clear who's the website is, I wouldn't go any further, I'd be suspicious – what have they got to hide?

- A clear, easy-to-follow structure, so that you do not get 'lost' when you are in it:

  ...not too much stuff, just simple pages with arrows telling you where to go next.

- Short, snappy facts and pieces of information that you can easily take away:

  ...most parents don't have time, you know, like for bookloads of stuff. Short and sweet is best I think.

- Images of black and Asian parents – this made many BME parents feel that the site was relevant to them, that the website might address issues for BME parents:

  If I see a black face then I'm more likely to think that that's for me, they've thought about me as a parent too.

  I saw the article on 'black dads' and immediately thought, 'yeah I'll go in there'.

- Having a date on the website (and in a clear place) to show when it was last updated:

  ...it really annoyed me [that website], like that all the stuff was two or three years old. No one would read a newspaper that old.

- Having a search engine on the website itself, which enabled parents to identify key words on the site:

  ...that's essential I think, so you can do, like we did, just put in 'bullying' or 'sex' or 'homework' or whatever. You have to have that.

- Quotes and articles from other parents, which reassured and made parents feel less alone:

> ...not all doom and gloom you know. Things from parents who've survived it.

- Having a specific button on the front page called 'Information for parents' or similar – this made parents feel that they were being invited to come in, that the organisation had thought through what parents needed:

> ...you do need to know that the website is for parents, or at least part of it is. If it's not for parents it should say so. If it is for parents you need to know that on the front page.

- Photographs and illustrations that reflect a wide range of families with different backgrounds – i.e. single parents as well as two-parent families, a range of ethnic groups, pictures of disabled children, young people and parents:

> ...that last one [website] we looked at, it was all happy families, 2.2 and all that. I'm a single mum and the website has to show that they know we're here too [laughs]!

- Making it clear on the front page whether you are in a British site, or an overseas one:

> We didn't realise for ages, did we, that that was American. We thought 'great they have free leaflets' [about alcohol] and then...ages later, realised it wasn't a British site. It really should say on the front page.

- Having information that clearly relates to young people of different ages – such as the DfES parents' website (www.parentingcentre.gov.uk), which has different age groupings:

> Look at this, this is great, I can go straight to the right age group for my son, no rooting around in the wrong section.

- Having a clear topic list so that if parents have a relatively common query, they can go straight there – an alphabetical list was preferred:

> ...it would help, like 'bullying', I can go straight to B and get the information, that's really helpful.

- Checklists relating to the question 'Is my child normal'?, i.e. easy-to-use guides to whether or not a parent should be concerned about something:

  > ...it sounds basic but I think that's what a lot of parents are looking for, just ticking off 'yes they do that, they don't do that', so that you know, should you be worried or not...

- Information in other languages for parents who do not have English as a first language – where this was not possible because of space, parents wanted a section that told parents where translated copies of the information could be obtained from:

  > ...this is important for me, as my English is not good, and it should have other languages on there.

- Having a detailed list of links to other organisations and their websites, including a brief summary of what each one provides:

  > ...[this one] is great, look at all those links to other organisations – you just click and you're there.

Conclusions

As stated earlier, many organisations involved in parenting support are now providing information and support via websites. Despite this rapid increase, there has been little opportunity to review website provision, and in particular little opportunity to find out about parents' views of this provision. That is what the project described in this chapter aimed to do.

A number of important findings came out of this research. As might be expected, parents had different views and experiences in relation to using websites. Some had little experience, whilst some had a considerable amount of experience. Whilst not a surprising finding, this does show how unwise it is to assume that websites are 'the way of the future'. For some parents this may not be the most appropriate form of help and support for them.

There were a number of other significant findings in the research. Most notable was the difficulties that most parents had in accessing information and advice on the internet. This was the case even for those parents who were very experienced at using the internet. This is a cause for concern. Whilst there is undoubtedly an enormous amount of valuable information for parents on the internet, most parents found it a frustrating and time-consuming experience to locate it.

It was also interesting that so many parents drifted towards two types of websites at some point – 'trusted' and 'well-known' ones such as the BBC's, and their child's school website. The fact that so many parents turned to school websites was an unexpected finding. However, it is also a problematic one, in that so many school websties do not contain any information about parenting issues. This could be addressed by having some standard sections and signposting on all school websites.

A number of recommendations can be made from this research. These relate to how websites are designed, structured and managed:

- Have an 'Information for parents' button, which acts as an 'invitation' to parents to enter the site – this helps parents to see that there is relevant information on the website for them.

- Ensure that the front page of the website states who the website has been provided by (i.e. the organisation concerned) and which country that organisation is based in.

- Do not insist that parents have to register.

- Have information provided clearly and simply, and in a variety of formats (articles, quizzes, short facts and 'tips', etc.).

- Have a detailed list of links to other organisations and their websites, including a brief summary of what each one provides.

- Specify on the website where information in other languages can be obtained from.

- Make it clear when the website was last updated.

- Have a keyword search which covers the whole website, not just part of it. Make sure the search feature is immediately visible.

- Include in the search engine (and on the website) a specific reference to 'black parenting' or 'BME parents'.

- Have both a list of topics that the website covers and an indication of the age ranges involved (for example, sections about babies, young children, teenagers, etc.).

- Ensure a diversity of photographs and illustrations, in particular by gender and by ethnicity. Many BME parents only feel 'welcomed' by a site if the designers show that they have thought about the diversity of parents they are trying to reach.

In concluding this chapter, readers should know that TSA has produced a 16-page Good Practice Guide, to help organisations to think through the way in which they approach providing information to parents via their website. This guide is now available from TSA.

Postscript

It is appropriate to close this chapter with a quote from one of the parents in the study, which highlights the potential that websites have as a form of information and support:

> Being a parent is so hard sometimes, and I have to say I've often felt really alone, really desperate. The stuff we've gone through today, all these websites, they're really REALLY good. I've been amazed, honestly. I just never knew all this was available. You really should tell people, you really should.

Learning for practitioners

- Whilst there has been a rapid rise in the use of websites as a way of supporting parents, we know little about whether this is meeting parents' needs.

- Many parents struggle to find the information and support they need on websites – helping parents to develop their search skills is essential.

- Organisations must design websites that are aimed at parents with particular care. Relatively small things can be off-putting and mean that a parent never returns. The list of things that parents like and dislike on websites are described in this chapter.

- Many parents expected to find parenting support information on school websites. Few schools, however, had any useful information. Adding some 'signposts' to school websites could be very valuable.

References

BCS (British Computer Society) (2004) *General IT Literacy: Research into the British Population and Computer Usage.* London: BCS.

Eysenbach, G. and Kohler, C. (2002) 'How do consumers search for and appraise health information on the world wide web?', *British Medical Journal 324,* 573–578.

Griffey, H. (2001) *Parenting Online.* London: NSPCC.

Loader, B. and Keeble, L. (2004) *Challenging the Digital Divide? A Review of Online Community Support.* York: Joseph Rowntree Foundation.

Williams, P., Nicholas, D., Huntington, P. and McClean, F. (2002) 'Surfing for health: user evaluation of a health information website.' *Health Information and Libraries Journal 19,* 2, 98–108.

10 Involving young people in parenting programmes

Cris Hoskin and Sarah Lindfield

This chapter describes learning from the Involving Young People in Parenting Programmes (IYPP) project, which was managed by the Trust for the Study of Adolescence (TSA). The IYPP project worked with five service delivery sites to deliver five different models of linking work with parents and young people. In this chapter we will outline the rationale for the IYPP project, report on the experiences of the young people, parents and staff involved and describe what we have learnt from the project development and delivery phases. It is not possible in this chapter to report on all the findings and lessons learnt from the project. However, the project report, which contains a full description of evaluation findings, can be found on the TSA website (Hoskin and Lindfield with Solanki and Hill 2005).

The rationale for the project

For many years there has been an acknowledgement of the links between offending and/or antisocial behaviour and family factors (see Loeber and Stouthamer-Loeber 1986 for a meta-analysis of research studies in this area). The Crime and Disorder Act (1998) introduced parenting orders. More recently, the Anti Social Behaviour Act (2003) and the Criminal Justice Act (2003) extended the original powers relating to parenting orders and introduced parenting contracts. The services that have been developed in this field have mainly focused on support to parents independently of interventions with their children. However, research in the US (Alexander, Holtzworth-Munroe and Jameson 1994; Kumpfer and Alvarado 1998; Mitchell, Weiss and Schultz 1993) has shown that work with both parents *and* children can be more effective than concentrating on just one or the other.

The IYPP project was designed as a small-scale study to learn more about how to provide linked services to parents and young people, to explore different models of service provision in this context and to provide learning to benefit others intending to develop their work with both parents and young people. The project was funded by the UK Treasury (under the Invest to Save Budget) and by the Youth Justice Board (YJB) for two years from 2002 to 2004.

The need for this type of project was identified recently in a review of international evidence in English-speaking countries on behalf of the Department for Education and Skills (Moran, Ghate and Van der Merwe 2004), which reported that:

> Similarly, to maximise the chances of affecting outcomes at the child behavioural level, parenting support programmes that have been most successful have worked directly with children as well as parents wherever possible, though again, not necessarily both at the same time. Again, the precise 'added value' of parallel working has yet to be established, however. Services that are making efforts to develop this type of working in the UK need to be given every support to do so, and enabled to carry out research on this specific aspect of service delivery and its impact. (p.119)

Project structure

The overall aim of the IYPP project was to:

> Develop and test effective practice models of involving young people in interventions, which strengthen parenting protective factors and reduce the parenting risk factors related to the offending/anti social behaviour/truancy of young people. (Hoskin *et al.* 2005, p.3)

In partnership with the YJB, the TSA provided the day-to-day management of the IYPP project. The TSA contracted with service deliverers to develop and test five models of involving young people in the interventions shown in Table 10.1.

Table 10.1: Models of intervention and the five delivery sites	
Model of intervention	**Delivery site**
Family therapy	Luton Youth Offending Team
Family skills training – strengthening families	Kinara Family Resource Centre, Greenwich
Parallel group programme	Centre for Fun and Families, Leicester
Family group conferencing	West Berkshire Family Group Conferencing Project
Parallel individual programme	East Berkshire Youth Offending Teams

The five models involved in the study were as follows:

Family therapy

Family therapy involves practitioners working with families either in their homes or in an office setting. The focus of the intervention is to improve family functioning, particularly in their ability to problem-solve an issue such as a family member's offending. The systems in which a family operates such as school, community, extended family and so on are explored. Issues are identified and unhelpful patterns of behaviour become the subject of a problem-solving approach to stimulate change. As many family members as possible explore the issues together, guided by the therapists. All referrals for the family therapy project were internal from Luton Youth Offending Team (YOT). The carers or parents were assessed for their need for support with regard to parenting skills or emotional help. The criteria for parents was that they should be caring for a young person (aged between 10 and 18 years), who was an open case to the YOT at the point of referral and had agreed to work on a voluntary basis.

Family skills training – strengthening families

This model consists of skills training for parents, children and families. Parents and children meet together at the beginning of each session for announcements. Following this, parents and children spend an hour in their respective groups. They then come together again and spend another hour in families. Refreshments are also provided but the timing varies. All referrals were via Greenwich Social Services Department. Parents were selected for the intervention if they had a young person aged 10–14 who had previously offended and/or were at risk of offending, were having difficulties within school and/or were at risk of exclusion, and if the parent and young person were willing to engage in some joint work.

Parallel group programme

Parallel groupwork involves a teenagers' group running at the same time as their parents' group, and covering the same core elements. Both groups will cover a range of topics including: communication, boundaries and discipline, problem-solving methods, conflict resolution and being a parent/being a teenager. The criteria for referral to the programme is that a parent/carer is experiencing difficulties in managing their teenager's behaviour leading to communication and relationship breakdown, for example, conflict, violence or aggression, refusal to follow rules/boundaries, school refusal, antisocial behaviour, offending behaviour. The referrals came through a range of services, with 42 per cent of the parents self-referring. Many of those who self-referred had been signposted to the service by other agencies.

Family group conferencing

Family group conferences are facilitated by an independent co-ordinator whose task is to bring together formal (professional/agency) and informal (family/community) networks in a collaborative decision-making process. At the conference, family outnumber the professionals and they will always have private family time (without any professionals present) to make a plan for the child. The aim is to empower families to take control of problems facing them and to share collective responsibility with professionals for resolving family difficulties. Referrals were sought and taken from the YOT, education and social services, and there was one referral for a health professional in a multidisciplinary team. The referral criteria mirrored that of the project as a whole, which was young people aged 10 to 17 at risk of school exclusion, truancy, bullying or behaviour problems at school or at risk of youth offending.

Parallel individual programme

Parallel individual work with teenagers covered core elements in tandem with their parents' programme. This involved joint working between parenting and youth justice workers to establish the pattern of the programme and topics covered. A mid-point and final review was held involving both workers and parent/s and teenagers, to discuss progress and consolidate their achievements. Referrals were taken from YOT staff, the police, education, social services and parents were also able to make self-referrals. The project was open to any parent/carer and their child/ young person between the ages of 10 and 17. The young people referred had to be involved in or be at risk of offending, displaying antisocial behaviour/challenging behaviour and/or had been missing from home or truanting from school.

Methods and sampling

The Policy Research Bureau (PRB), an independent research centre, coordinated and managed the evaluation element of the IYPP project and evaluated its success in achieving the aim of the project. The information gathered was used to evaluate the processes involved in implementing the different interventions and the experiences of parents and young people.

Data was collected from young people, parents and delivery-site workers using quantitative and in-depth qualitative methods. Parents and young people were asked to complete questionnaires before or at the start of their intervention, and again at the end ('Before' and 'After' questionnaires). Project workers also completed questionnaires about their perceptions of the experiences of young people and parents involved in the project at the end of the intervention, including parents and young people who had not fully completed the intervention. Additionally, individual interviews were held with eight young people, ten parents and five delivery-site workers (one per site).

We describe below some of the key findings from the project evaluation. In total 127 families took part in the IYPP project but not all of these families were included in the study sample. Some parents and young people chose not to complete the questionnaires. Also, there were low numbers of families where both parents took part and completed questionnaires (13 families) and so no meaningful comparison between mothers' and fathers' experiences could be carried out. Therefore, the PRB included only the mothers' questionnaires as main carers from these families to match the majority of the sample who were mothers. Thirteen fathers who took part in the project and completed questionnaires were therefore not included in the study sample.

Parent sample

The 'Before' questionnaires were completed by 119 parents, the majority of whom were white British. Seventy-three of these parents also completed 'After' questionnaires. Additionally, four parents completed only 'After' questionnaires. Eighteen parents dropped out or did not complete the intervention. The majority of parents were mothers, with just five fathers included in the study sample as the main carer. The PRB interviewed ten parents after the intervention, two from each service delivery site and all were mothers.

Young people sample

The 'Before' questionnaires were completed by 104 young people, the majority of whom were white British. Sixty-one of these young people also completed 'After' questionnaires. Additionally, four young people completed only 'After' questionnaires. Twenty-one young people dropped out or did not complete the intervention. Of the 104 young people, 60 were boys and 44 girls and were aged between 10 and 17 years. Most were between 11 and 15 years old. The PRB interviewed eight young people individually at the end of the project.

Learning about parents' and young people's experiences
Expectations of the project

Parents and young people were asked to rate their expectations of the project in the 'Before' questionnaire. They were also asked to complete a similar question at the end of the project, in the 'After' questionnaire, to identify whether their expectations had been met.

Overall, parents and young people expected the project to be helpful, with 99 per cent of parents (from a total of 73) and just under three-quarters of the young people (from a total of 61) expecting the project to be helpful to them. At the end of the project the results were very similar, suggesting that the expectations of the majority of parents and of young people had been met. Of the remainder, one young person who had expected the project not to be helpful had found it helpful, whereas a few young people who had expected to find it helpful rated it neutrally ('neither helpful nor unhelpful'). One young person who had positive expectations at the start of the project said that they had found it 'very unhelpful'.

Satisfaction with the project

In order to assess satisfaction with different aspects of the project, parents and young people were asked a number of questions on the 'After' questionnaire about the intervention and the workers and to rate different aspects on a six-point scale as 'very true', 'fairly true', 'neither true nor untrue', 'fairly untrue', 'very untrue' or 'can't say'. They were asked to comment on whether the project was interesting and whether the workers knew what they were doing, understood how they were feeling and listened to what they were saying. The number of parents answering these questions was 69 and young people 65.[1] The results can be seen in Table 10.2.

Overall, parents and young people were very satisfied with different aspects of the projects, as can be seen from Table 10.2. They found the interventions interesting and felt that the staff knew what they were doing, understood how they felt and listened to what they had to say.

It is interesting, however, to note some differences between the views of parents and young people in the study sample. Parents were overwhelmingly positive about each of these aspects of the project, whereas young people's responses were slightly more varied. Fewer young people than parents rated each of the statements as 'very true' and a few young people did not find the project interesting, or felt that the staff were competent or felt that the staff understood them. The two areas in

---

1   Except for whether staff 'knew what they were doing', when 64 young people responded.

Table 10.2: Parents' and young people's satisfaction with aspects of the project (%)

Statement	Rating of 'very true' or 'fairly true'	
	Parents	Young people
The project was interesting	97	86
The project workers knew what they were doing	100	94
The project workers understood how the parent/young person was feeling	99	84
The project workers listened to what the parent/young person had to say	100	96

particular that young people rated less positively than parents, were in finding the project interesting and feeling that the workers understood how they were feeling.

Parents' and young people's perceptions of change

Overall parents who completed 'Before' and 'After' questionnaires[2] were found to have experienced:

- improved communication with their child/young person
- some improvement in levels of conflict with their young person
- improved overall sense of coping
- improved warmth towards their young person
- increased feeling of being able to supervise their young person.

2   Between 66 and 69 parents responded to questions in these sections of the 'Before' and 'After' questionnaires.

Overall, young people who completed 'Before' and 'After' question-naires[3] were found to have experienced:

- a slight deterioration in communication (overall) with their parents
- slightly less conflict with mothers, but no change with fathers
- slight reduction in numbers of times young people were involved in antisocial behaviour, offending and truancy, and in the numbers of young people involved in antisocial behaviour, offending and truancy
- little change in warmth overall (although a slight improvement in warmth from mothers).

Overall then, parents responding to these sections of the 'Before' and 'After' questionnaires experienced significant positive changes. For young people there was not much change overall. In a few cases, young people's behaviour had deteriorated during the course of the intervention. However, as we have highlighted above, we cannot relate these positive and negative changes directly to involvement in the project, as there are other factors that may have influenced them.

One factor that emerged from the individual interviews with parents and young people was that some of the families involved had multiple issues to contend with, such as truancy, conflict within the family and offending behaviour. It may be that the interventions provided in the IYPP project should be offered as part of a package of interventions to deal with these multiple issues and/or that the intensity of the intervention should match the level of difficulty a family is experiencing.

The project staff at each delivery site were also asked to complete questionnaires at the end of each parent's and young person's intervention. Ninety-seven questionnaires were completed by staff. Although staff perception was that families had benefited overall, they also thought that parents had benefited slightly more than young people. Additionally, five staff were interviewed individually (one from each site) and all of

---

3   Between 57 and 59 young people responded to questions in these sections of the 'Before' and 'After' questionnaires, except that between 41 and 50 young people responded to the questions on antisocial behaviour, offending and truancy.

them were positive about this way of working. Views from individual staff members included the following:

- Individual direct work can be made more meaningful by bringing parents and young people together.

- The emphasis on the parent–child relationship when both worked together had a positive impact on parents' engagement.

- For some families it is an opportunity to spend time with each other.

- Working together gave young people the opportunity to have a voice in the process of looking at family relationships.

Learning from the development phase

As with the implementation of any new piece of work, a number of issues emerged for the service delivery sites. The four main areas are discussed below.

Length of the development phase

One of the key selection criteria for the service delivery sites in the IYPP project was that they already delivered services to parents. Some had already begun to develop linked work with young people and parents, even if they were still at the early planning stages. Each of the projects selected therefore had a good platform from which to develop. A development phase was built in to the IYPP project as a whole in recognition of the work involved in implementing the project in each site. Each of the service delivery sites had an individualised delivery phase, lasting between three and six months, dependent upon individual issues. However, in retrospect it emerged that even where existing service provision was well established, the development phase was not long enough as reported by the service delivery sites in the individual inter-views with staff at the end of the project. The main reasons for this were staff recruitment, staff training, sorting out logistical and resource issues and establishing relationships with other agencies. Anyone wishing to develop similar services should allow sufficient time to address these issues and include contingency time for unexpected events such as key staff leaving.

Referrals

In all the service delivery sites, changes were made to the referral processes in order to improve the flow and appropriateness of the referrals. The reasons for this included:

- referrers who did not understand the service and only referred parents

- low numbers of referrals

- referrals of families with complex needs such as parents with severe mental health issues.

The delivery sites addressed these issues in a range of ways: through training sessions with colleagues about the nature and aims of the service, attending team meetings to provide information and updates on the project, the development of publicity material describing the project and through direct case discussion with referrers.

Resource implications

It is vital that the resources required to implement new ways of working are addressed early on during the development phase of project work. Different models of intervention will have different resource implications and the following questions need to be answered before the delivery phase:

- *What are the minimum and optimum staffing levels?* In the IYPP project the minimum staffing levels varied from one (family group conferencing) to three (family skills training).

- *What training do staff need?* This again varied in the IYPP project. Some of the models of intervention, such as family therapy, family group conferencing and family skills training require training in the methodology to be able to deliver. For parallel group and parallel individual programmes, training may be needed in co-working and/or groupwork skills and in delivering a specific programme. This will depend upon the staff in place or recruited.

- *Venues and other programme resources* Some issues were common to other models of intervention (such as the provision of transport, child care and refreshments) to support participation and engagement. In addition, the provision of sufficient administrative support was important. In the IYPP project, all the service delivery sites needed to think carefully about finding appropriate venues for their mode of delivery. Issues varied from finding venues large enough to accommodate large groups of people, to finding suitable alternative venues to families' homes in the evenings.

Management and partnership arrangements

Strong partnership working is desirable for a number of reasons, such as sharing resources, avoiding duplication of work and ensuring that different agencies with the same client group work towards common aims, objectives and outcomes. In the IYPP project there were various partnership arrangements across the five models of intervention. The project evaluation found that there were successful examples of partnership arrangements, but that in some cases there were difficulties, such as agreeing protocols in relation to confidentiality and information sharing that needed to be addressed. Maintaining good communication was key to successful partnership working and this could be affected if, for example, key staff left and new relationships had to be established.

Management support for staff supervision is clearly important for the effective delivery of all services. The site delivery staff in the IYPP project all felt that the issue of supervision was more complex than in other areas of their work, mainly due to the fact that most of the workers were co-facilitators or working with both parent and young person. Supervision was the topic of a workshop facilitated by TSA, and is discussed in more detail below.

Learning from practice

Throughout the life of the IYPP project, the project coordinator facilitated multi-site meetings, which were attended by representatives from the five service delivery sites. The purpose of these meetings was to identify and discuss common practice issues and themes shared across the different models of intervention. The common themes were identified at the first multi-site meeting and were used to set the agenda for subsequent meetings. The nature of each meeting varied according to the focus, and included training, workshops, practice forums or discussion groups. A number of issues also emerged during the delivery phase of the project and these were added to the initial agenda items.

The main themes that emerged during the course of the IYPP project were issues of confidentiality, joint or separate sessions for parents and young people, starting work with parents before working with young people, involving fathers and supervision. These are explored further below.

Confidentiality

Confidentiality has been mentioned previously in relation to information sharing within partnership arrangements. Here, we mean the confidentiality contract or agreement between a worker and each family member. Whilst issues of confidentiality should always be addressed when working with families, the fact that in all cases the IYPP project was working with more than one family member brought additional complexities. This was the case whether or not the same staff worked with the parent(s) as well as their young person.

The project evaluation found that both parents and young people had concerns about confidentiality issues. Staff also reported in the multi-site meetings that young people appeared to be less willing to be open with information in the group setting, in case the information was shared with their parents. This was especially true when the same workers were facilitating a group for their (the young people's) parents. Some parents wanted to know what the young people were saying in their (parallel) sessions. Some parents were also concerned that the young people may say things in their parallel group that other young people could pass on to parents with whom they were sharing a group. At times this may become an issue for workers who are working with parents as well as their children/young people, as it may sometimes seem useful to share information that may enhance understanding between the two, and yet this has not been agreed.

Workers should be aware of these issues and can address them by:

- developing clear confidentiality protocols and information-sharing agreements

- preparing some examples that can be used to illustrate issues and sharing them with family members to enhance understanding

- having good knowledge of and clear procedures regarding child protection issues

- identifying and agreeing non-negotiable areas

- addressing confidentiality issues with parents and young people separately and together and setting ground rules at the beginning of the intervention.

Sessions for parents and young people – joint or separate?

In the IYPP project there were five different models of intervention, two of which involved parents and young people working together (family therapy and family group conferencing), two of which had parents and young people working in parallel (parallel group and parallel individual programmes) and in the case of family skills training a mixture of joint sessions bringing parents and young people together, and parallel sessions in separate parents' groups and young people's groups.

Interviews with staff and with ten parents and eight young people revealed that some adaptation of the models of intervention delivered could be beneficial. Where young people were working in interventions with their parents, they may have benefited from additional separate sessions. As this young person said:

> I like it when my mum's with us because then she can hear what I'm saying, she'll understand it. But there's some things I would like just to talk about with just some other person that actually understands me.

Conversely, in the separate but parallel models, parents and young people may have benefited from having some joint sessions where they worked together. Some parents commented, for example, that they did not really know what the young person was doing in their programme. Some young people felt that working with their parents provided an opportunity to spend time together and one young person felt that it meant his family could understand his feelings better. Other young people preferred to work with their peers rather than their parents. Clearly, the issue of how best to structure these models could benefit from further exploration.

Working with parents first

One factor that emerged for projects working in parallel (parallel group and parallel individual programmes) was whether the parents' and young people's sessions should start at the same time or be staggered. Initially the sites involved started the sessions at the same time. After a short period of time, however, both sites began the parents' sessions *before* the young people's sessions. In both cases this was thought to be more effective as it gave the parents the opportunity to 'get things off their chest' (quote from a worker at a multi-site meeting). The sites felt that by starting work with the parents first they were beginning to work on parenting issues and parents might therefore be able to support their young person better when they began their programme. Interestingly, the two sites independently decided to stagger their start dates by working with the parents for *three weeks* before working with the young people.

The family skills training model involved parallel groups and family time. The experience at this site was, however, similar to those who were offering parallel work and the site also decided to offer three introductory sessions to parents prior to the main intervention. This was felt to be particularly useful where the parents had not been involved in previous interventions. For anyone wishing to offer parallel work with parents and young people, this issue should be considered carefully at the planning and development phases.

Involving fathers

Overall, the numbers of fathers taking part in the project were low. Of the parents who took part in the IYPP project and completed 'Before' questionnaires, only 18 were fathers compared to 114 mothers. A recent review by Moran *et al.* (2004) stated that it is still the case that 'relatively few studies discuss or analyse fathers as a specific group' (p.103). They suggest that rather than having an understanding of what works in parenting, we 'mainly know about supporting mothers' (p.128). The limited numbers in the evaluation element of the IYPP project did not allow us to investigate or comment upon the experiences of fathers involved in the interventions. Clearly, however, there is a case for more research about involving fathers in future evaluations and studies, as well as continuing to make efforts to involve fathers in parenting interventions.

Supervision

During the IYPP project the issue of staff supervision arose on a number of occasions. All the delivery-site workers had supervision in the workplace in line with their agency's supervision policy and procedures. The inclusion of young people in parenting interventions raised additional issues that could be addressed in supervision. In many cases, for example, more than one worker was involved and in all cases more than one family member was involved. The range of types of supervision suitable for a number of different purposes is addressed in the IYPP project report, where the advantages and disadvantages of a range of supervision methods are detailed.

The site delivery staff participated in a workshop to discuss the supervision issues that had arisen in the IYPP project. A model of supervision for work with families was developed from this workshop and is described in Box 10.1.

Conclusions

The five models of intervention in the IYPP project offer ways of linking direct work with young people and parents. There are, however, other ways in which parenting service providers can widen their work to ensure that it encompasses the needs of the whole family and in particular of children and young people. Additionally, services aimed at young people can look for ways to involve parents in their young person's intervention. We see this two-way process as operating along a continuum of provision, where methods and intensity of parenting support and the young person's support are matched to levels of need. At one end of the spectrum, the young person could be involved in the parenting assessment process and take part in one or more parenting sessions. Similarly, parents should be encouraged to support any interventions for the young person. At the other end of the spectrum there is a need for long-term, intensive family interventions. In between, there is a myriad of possibilities. What is clear is that services have a range of options along the continuum to cater for the diverse needs of service users.

Box 10.1: Supervision model

Site staff agreed that the following elements of supervision should be in place:

1. *Line management* – agency driven and dealing with accountability, etc.

2. *Clinical/reflective supervision* – could be done within line management or as a separate process and with a different person.

3. *Additionally* (and depending upon the intervention model) one or more of the following supervision methods should be available:

    a. *Consultancy* – for groups (beginning, middle and end of each group), for individual work or workers (at an agreed frequency). One of the project sites delivering groups, had consultation sessions at the beginning, middle and end points of the group process.

    b. *Planning and debriefing sessions* – as co-facilitators of a group or as separate workers working with the same family, as in parallel individual work.

    c. *Peer supervision/practice forum* – can be within own agency/service or across agencies.

The final point to make is that the IYPP as a pilot project did have some limitations, such as low numbers involved and the lack of a control group. A more detailed discussion of the limitations can be found in the IYPP project report. It has, however, highlighted the need for a full research study in this area, involving comparison groups and a larger number of families, as we do not yet know:

- the effectiveness of different models of intervention
- outcomes over a longer time period

- whether positive outcomes for young people and parents can be attributed to particular interventions

- whether the findings for the parents and young people in this study would be the same for other parents and young people.

Learning for practitioners

- Practitioners linking work with parents and young people will ideally be able to draw on a range of approaches, along a continuum from low-level to more intensive models.

- An adequate development phase should be built in to planning for a new or extended service.

- As with any new service, referral procedures need to be clearly defined and colleagues given repeated opportunities to learn about the nature and aims of the service. This will help to ensure a good flow of appropriate referrals to the project.

- A range of supervision opportunities can be identified to support practitioners to address some of the complex issues that can emerge.

- The majority of parents and young people involved in the IYPP project were very satisfied with different aspects of the project. However, some young people did not find the project interesting or feel understood by the workers.

- Clear procedures should be established in relation to confidentiality, and a confidentiality agreement established with parents and young people.

- Practitioners should consider offering joint sessions where parents and young people are involved in separate parallel programmes and separate sessions when they are working together.

References

Alexander, J.F., Holtzworth-Munroe, A. and Jameson, P.B. (1994) 'The process and outcome of marital family therapy.' In A.E. Bergin and S.L. Garlfield (eds) *Handbook of Psychotherapy and Behavioural Change.* New York: John Wiley.

Hoskin, C. and Lindfield, S. with Solanki, A.-R. and Hill, E. (2005) *Involving Young People in Parenting Programmes Project Report.* Brighton: Trust for the Study of Adolescence.

Kumpfer, K.L. and Alvarado, R. (1998) 'Effective family strengthening interventions.' *Juvenile Justice Bulletin November 1998.* Washington, DC: Office of Juvenile Justice and Delinquency Prevention, US Department of Justice.

Kumpfer, K.L. and Turner, C.W. (1991) 'The social ecology model of adolescence substance abuse: implications for prevention.' *The International Journal of Addictions, 25*, 4A, 435–63.

Loeber, R. and Stouthamer-Loeber, M. (1986) 'Family factors as correlates and predictors of juvenile conduct problems and delinquency.' In M. Morris and M. Tony (eds) *Crime and Justice: Vol. 7.* Chicago, IL: University of Chicago Press.

Mitchell, A., Weiss, H. and Schultz, T. (1993) *Evaluating Education Reform: Early Childhood Education. A Review of Research on Early Education, Family Support and Parent Education.* Alexandria, VA: National Association of State Boards of Education.

Moran, P., Ghate, D. and Van der Merwe, A. (2004) *What Works in Parenting Support? A Review of the International Evidence.* Research Report 574. London: Home Office and Department for Education and Skills.

11 Using parent-to-parent mentors to get information and support to the parents of young people

Debi Roker

Over the last few years, mentoring has been a key method used in promoting support and interpersonal development. This mentoring has taken place in two main ways, either adults mentoring young people, or young people acting as peer mentors to other young people. Although there is not a very good evidence base for this, anecdotal evidence suggests that mentoring can provide support and personal development for both 'sides' of the equation. One reason for this is said to be that many people feel more comfortable with another 'person' rather than a 'professional'. Inevitably, professionals and practitioners are in positions of power and authority, and often have a certain degree of control over the relationship. Peer mentoring is seen to offer a form of support which makes relationships more 'equal'.

In 2001 the national children's charity, the National Council for Voluntary Child Care Organisations (NCVCCO), secured funding to run a pilot programme, to explore the use of mentoring in relation to parenting. The aim was to pilot the use of 'parent-to-parent' mentoring, i.e. parents supporting each other during times of difficulty. The aim of the pilot project was to set up mentoring schemes, to enable parents of secondary school-age children to help support parents of younger children, especially around the transition to secondary school. The Trust for the Study of Adolescence (TSA) was contracted to undertake the evaluation of this initiative. The outcomes and learning from the project are described in this chapter.

There has been an increased number of projects in recent years that use mentoring as a way of teaching and/or supporting people. Despite this increased prevelance, however, this form of support has not been widely used in relation to parenting. The NCVCCO secured a grant from the Department for Education and Skills to run a three-year pilot project. The aim was to look at the effectiveness of mentoring as a form of support for parents of children and young people.

The project

The NCVCCO worked with three partner sites on this project, as follows (using pseudonyms):

- Marston Training, Humberside: this project involved an independent training and counselling organisation. The company provides a range of services for families, including running a number of 'parenting teenagers' courses. Two staff were involved in the parent mentoring project.

- Cornerways Resource Centre, London: this centre is run by social services and provides a variety of services including group-based parenting courses and one-to-one work. It works closely with the local Youth Offending Team (YOT).

- Yardley Family Centre, in collaboration with the local social services department, Cambridgeshire: this centre provides a range of services for families in the area. The parent mentoring project was a collaboration between the charity and the local social services department. Both Yardley Family Centre and social services provided the time of an experienced family worker.

The NCVCCO provided some financial support for each project. Each site was given a grant of £2500 for each of the three years, i.e. £7500 over the course of the project. This was intended to cover some aspects of the project only, and it was not seen as covering such things as the staff time needed to run a parent mentoring project.

The broad aim of each of the projects was to recruit and train a number of parents at each of the three sites, who would become 'parent mentors'. It was proposed that these would be parents of older young people (i.e. 12- to 15-year-olds), including those who had experienced problems in their own parenting and parent–child relationships. It was further proposed that the 'mentees', who would be recruited in a variety of ways, would ideally be those with children aged 8 to 12. Thus, the ambition was to have parents of secondary-age children support those with primary-age children.

The emphasis of the parent mentoring project was very much on trying out different approaches and experimenting with different ways of working, in order to find out what works and what doesn't (or at least what is promising practice and what isn't). The three sites above were therefore selected in order to explore how parent mentoring schemes work in different settings – i.e. a family/community centre, a large children's charity in collaboration with social services, and a private training organisation.

TSA's research

There were two broad aims of TSA's evaluation of this pilot initiative, as follows:

- To identify the *impact and outcomes* of parent mentoring schemes on mentors and mentees. The aim was to identify whether the projects had an effect on parents' levels of knowledge and understanding, confidence, perceptions of support and consideration of different options for dealing with difficult issues or situations with their children.

- To identify the *processes* involved in setting up and running parent mentoring projects. This included the successes of the projects, any difficulties and challenges that arose and the main learning points that could be of use to others in the future. Thus, it was considered important to secure feedback from all those involved – mentors, mentees and project workers.

A variety of data was collected at each site, involving telephone and face-to-face interviews with project workers, mentors and mentees. As is explained later, relatively few 'pairings' took place in the projects, so few mentees were interviewed. The interviews took place over a two-and-a-half-year period, with many participants interviewed four or five times.

The main results are presented below, focusing on the views of project workers first, then the mentors and mentees.

Project workers' views and experiences

The development of the project at each site, and the experiences of the project workers, are detailed below.

Humberside

At the Humberside site, following the completion of a 'parenting teenagers' course run at the site, a number of parents were identified as potential mentors to take part in the NCVCCO project. These mentors then undertook an additional course to train as mentors. The mentoring course was designed by the two project workers, in collaboration with the parents. Although seven mentors were involved in the training, a core group of three mentors were maintained throughout the life of the project.

The aim of the Humberside project was to offer the parent mentoring service to primary schools in the local area, as a mentor–mentee telephone support service. The aim was therefore to pair the mentors with parents of primary school-aged children who were experiencing difficulties, or who had concerns about their child's move to secondary school. A wide variety of advertising materials and contacts was developed in order to promote the parent mentoring project. However, despite a considerable amount of effort by the project workers, no mentees were referred by local schools. A wide range of activities was developed, however, to keep the mentors engaged during this period – this included ongoing training events, social activities and designing advertising materials for the parent mentoring project.

Although by the end of the evaluation period no mentees had been involved in the project, the project is (at the time of writing) still ongoing and alternative avenues to reach parents are being explored. The project workers and the mentors are hopeful that they will still be able to recruit mentees to the project. In addition, there have been a number of unexpected 'spin-offs' from the project and a great deal of positive learning. These are explored below.

One of the key themes that came through from the two Humberside workers was the amount of time and energy put into both the training of the mentors and the recruitment of mentees. In terms of attracting mentees to the project, the brief description above does not do justice to the numbers of telephone calls, visits to schools, fliers prepared, etc. that were involved to advertise the project. A key theme that emerged was the time that making and developing these contacts takes, even when some of the 'groundwork' has already been done via previous contact. As one of the workers explained:

> ...it really needs time, a long time to build up those links and relationships. It can't be done overnight.

Linked to this point, another theme that came through strongly was the need to focus on keeping the mentors involved. The three main mentors in the project did stay (and indeed still are) involved. Again this took considerable time and effort, involving the project workers in organising ongoing training and other events, to keep them motivated. For example:

> ...we've been to the theatre, had dinner, kept them together as a group. That's been really important for morale, for keeping them going...

One of the issues that emerged strongly from the interviews with the Humberside project workers, was ways in which the project can be developed for the future. At the time of the last interview, for example, the workers had started to diversify the project in new and interesting ways. This included having a parents' drop-in at a local health centre, which was proving promising. This two-hour drop-in, run every Friday morning, was already attracting parents. The original group of mentors may get involved in this in the future, and develop it more along the lines of the HOPE (Hands On Parenting Extra) drop-in at the London site – see below.

In addition, a key unexpected outcome was that the mentors had become involved in 'informal mentoring'. Thus, the mentors had become known in their workplaces, and amongst their friends, as people that parents could talk to about parenting issues. This often happened during general work events, during lunchtimes and in social settings. Whilst the project workers had not anticipated this being a part of the project, it did in fact seem to be tapping a real need. As the workers said:

> ...it's mentoring on the spot, addressing issues when parents have a problem and they feel safe to talk, it's great.

> [Mentoring has] become normalised in coffee breaks and lunch breaks, it's just part of general conversations and interactions.

In addition to helping parents with problems, this informal mentoring also allowed the mentors to practise their skills and feel engaged in the mentoring role. Thus, as well as establishing the drop-in (mentioned above), the project workers felt that it would be worth developing this more informal aspect of mentoring.

Cambridgeshire

The project workers at the Cambridgeshire site secured a group of mentors, by approaching all those involved on a parenting course that they ran. Four individuals subsequently trained as mentors, although one later left the area, leaving a core group of three. The project workers designed their own training course for the mentors, which took place over four half-day sessions. The topics covered included listening skills, boundaries, the needs of 8- to 11-year-olds etc. In order for the mentors to work as part of the national charity in which the project took place, they needed to be taken on as volunteers. This required them to have Criminal Record Bureau (CRB) checks, a medical and sign up to a code of conduct. Although time-consuming, this also gave them the full support of the volunteer staff system.

During the mentoring training process, the group also explored how to advertise for and work with mentees. It was agreed in the early stages that the contact between mentor and mentee would be face to face – this was mainly because of the physical isolation of many parents who live in the rural area concerned. It was thus felt that face-to-face contact was a key part of the process.

Advertising material was also prepared by the mentors in collabora-tion with the project workers. This was sent to local primary and second-ary schools, in an effort to get referrals to the service. However, during the evaluation period only two mentees became involved with a mentor. (One of these was interviewed by the author and their views are detailed in the next section.) Securing mentees was made more difficult because of the closure of the host project part way through the project.

Many of the comments made by the two Cambridgeshire project workers reflected those of the Humberside workers (above). Both of the Cambridgeshire workers felt that the development and training of their mentors had gone well and that the core group of mentors had a lot to offer:

> ...they're the experts now, they really are. They're very good, they can really do this well.

> ...I feel really positive, very positive about them, they've got a lot to offer other parents.

However, there was clearly disappointment over the lack of referrals to the project. It was considered that there was a variety of reasons for this, including sudden changes at local schools (such as amalgamation) and the plans of some organisations to refer 'inappropriate' parents (such as those in crisis or needing specialist help). Towards the end of the evaluation period, however, three appropriate referrals were made and mentors and mentees were paired. As one worker said, this was a very positive moment:

> ...that made all the difference, we felt we'd taken off, something good had happened.

One of these three mentees has an ongoing relationship with a mentor, and the other two mentees have occasional contact when they feel they need it. The feedback from one of these mentees is given later in this chapter.

One other development took place at the Cambridgeshire site towards the end of the project. The workers have been involved in setting up a new mentoring project in a nearby town. This has involved recruiting and training a new group of mentors. The two groups of 'old' and 'new' mentors are now getting together at regular intervals to share ideas and experiences. It is considered that the learning from the first project will help to develop and improve how the new project is run. As one of the workers commented:

> ...we learnt a great deal from the first one, it's really helping the new one get off the ground.

It should also be noted that there have been other 'spin-offs' from the first project for the mentors concerned. Some have become involved in other related activities, such as giving presentations to groups of parents and doing volunteer mentoring at the local YOT. Significantly – reflecting the experiences of mentors in the Humberside project (above) – several of the mentors have also been involved in informal mentoring. Thus, they have provided informal advice and support, mainly to friends and their work colleagues. This is an important avenue for future work.

London

At the London site, parents were approached to train as mentors who had attended one of the centre's parenting courses. Five parents completed the training. An external consultant was used to run the mentoring training, using an already devised training manual. Another four parents were then recruited and trained from a second course. A key issue that arose early on for the London site, was that for the mentors to work unsupervised with parents, they needed to have completed their CRB checks. At the time, this was taking up to a year for some parents. Thus, it was decided to engage the mentors in others activities during this period. This included, for example, speaking to groups of parents about their experiences of attending a group-based course.

Crucially, the parents and the workers also set up HOPE (Hands On Parenting Extra), a drop-in service for local parents. This drop-in then became the focus of the mentors' work. It was staffed on a rota basis by the mentors, and attracted small numbers of parents on a regular basis. Some only came in once and discussed an issue in relation to their parenting. Others came in on a regular basis, looking for longer-term help and support. The service was advertised widely, in general practitioner surgeries, the police station, schools, shops, etc.

Overall, the two workers at the London site felt that the parent mentoring project had worked well. They considered that they had adapted to the situations they found themselves in, for example setting up HOPE as an alternative to one-to-one mentoring. They also considered that the training had worked well and that the parents involved in HOPE were aware of needs and boundaries and able to refer on to them (as project managers) if any difficulties arose. For example:

> …we've spent a lot of time on key things, like child protection. They know the agreed rules, and they keep to them.

The workers thus considered that the volunteers provided a very valuable service to other parents. They were able to listen, talk through options, identify additional sources of help and support and follow up where necessary. The workers thought it was particularly valuable that the parents were able to demonstrate that they had also had difficulties with their children and young people, but had 'got through it'. For example:

> …it is reassuring for the other parent [the mentee] to know that, you know, here's someone who's been through it, who's been there themselves.

One of the other issues raised by the project workers was the impact of being mentors on the mentors themselves. One described their project as:

> …a victim of our own success – they've really developed and they move on, which is great of course, at one level…

This worker explained that, as a result of the training and experiences they have, the mentors often wish to move on to other things. Thus, one mentor, for example, secured paid work; others returned to study. As a result of this, many of the mentors were no longer able to commit to providing volunteer support at HOPE, or get involved in other work. The parent mentoring project thus enabled people to develop new skills and develop their personal and career plans. Whilst this was welcomed, it also had a knock-on effect on the project, in that experienced mentors were no longer available and needed to be replaced.

Mentors' and mentees' views and experiences

This section describes the views and experiences of the parent mentors and the mentees separately.

Mentors

In total, 11 mentors were involved in interviews, some on one occasion only, and some on up to three occasions. The mentors were drawn from all three projects. Their views and experiences are combined here, as there was considerable overlap in what was said. The main themes that came out of these interviews were as follows:

WHY THEY BECAME INVOLVED

There was one reason in particular that parents gave for wanting to train as mentors – this was that, having experienced problems and difficulties themselves, they wanted to 'give something back'. As these parents described it:

> ...I felt, well, I've been through it, some really bad stuff, really hard times...and I wanted to show other people, say to them 'look at me, you can get through it, even when you're really despairing', so yes that's why, to give something back in a way.

> ...we had a really hard time with our son and I thought 'what a good idea', we didn't have anyone 'til we came on the course, so, yes, to help other parents.

> ...I thought I'd like to help other people not make the same mistakes I did, to learn from my mistakes.

In addition to wanting to give something back, however, parents mentioned some other reasons. The most common ones centred on wanting to develop new skills and abilities that might lead on to new volunteering or employment opportunities. For example:

> ...as well I did think, you know, it would look good when I was going for jobs, once I go back to work, you know on my CV.

> I think I've learnt a lot of skills, it will help me get a better job, to say I've done this.

WHAT THE MENTOR ROLE INVOLVES

The role of the mentor was described by the parents in a wide variety of ways. However, the most common descriptions centred on 'listening' and 'support'. For example:

> ...to listen, just listen and let people talk, letting them know someone cares.

> …supporting them is really important. You can't change things for them, but you can, sort of, help them through it, provide support.

> …be there for them, be a good friend really.

In addition, the mentor role was seen to involve talking through different options, and helping people to get other support if they needed it:

> …we talk things through, you know the kind of thing, 'well you could do this, or you could do that, but if you do this that might happen' sort of thing. Just going through options with people.

> I stress their strengths, and say 'stick with that'. I tell all parents they've done something right, or tried really hard at something…well, that's important.

> …we have a list of phone numbers and services, sometimes we just go through that, in that they need to speak to someone else.

POSITIVE ASPECTS OF MENTORING

All of the mentors were very positive about their role and felt that mentoring had a great deal to offer other parents. It was considered particularly valuable for those parents who were alone, or unsupported, or 'at the end of their tether'. As explained above, the parents felt that they could provide a listening ear, but also help parents to look at alternatives and options. They were also able to signpost parents towards other forms of help and advice, where necessary. Crucially, however, they could show that other people get through it:

> I think of myself as a survivor [laughs]…yes I do, really, because I got through it. There were times [with my son] when I felt so low, but I'm still here now, and things are better, and I tell people that – that it will get better.

DIFFICULTIES AND CHALLENGES IN THE ROLE/PROJECT

There were a relatively small number of challenges and difficulties in the projects that the mentors mentioned. Many of these have already come up in the earlier sections of this chapter. This included, for example, having to wait a long time for CRB checks to come through and thus having to change the nature of the support offered. A key issue was also the difficulties involved in recruiting the mentees to the projects and feeling that their skills and expertise were to a certain extent being wasted. For example:

> ...yeah it has been frustrating...you know we're here [laughs], we're ready to go [laughs], we'd all really like to get on with putting it all into practice.

In addition the mentors mentioned the difficulties of not getting too involved, and remaining detached. For example:

> ...seeing someone cry, it's hard not to cry too, it really is.

However, all the mentors (at all three sites) commented on how both the training they had received, and the back-up from the project workers, enabled them to deal with difficult circumstances like this. The high level of support received from all six project workers was something that came up repeatedly in the interviews with the mentors.

Mentees

As described above, only one mentee was interviewed, from the Cambridgeshire project. However, in addition, some parents who visited the HOPE project in the London site were also briefly spoken to, to get some feedback about their experiences. These results are detailed in this section.

First, the mentee who was interviewed had been involved with a mentor for five months or so. Her daughter had been truanting regularly and relationships had become difficult between them. She had been put in touch with the parent mentoring project via an outreach worker at her child's school. She was attracted to the service because she wanted to talk things through with someone and decide what she could do to improve things with her daughter. Having been put in contact with one of the mentors in the Cambridgeshire project, they began to meet regularly.

This mother was extremely positive about the mentoring scheme, and how it had helped her:

> [the main thing]...was just having someone there, to talk things through.

In addition, this mentee commented on how helpful it was to talk through different options for dealing with her daughter and their relationship, and getting someone else's perspective on the issue. This mother added that, by the time of the interview, there had been no change in her daughter's behaviour. However, having the support of the mentor meant that she felt able to '...keep battling on...'. As she explained it:

> I couldn't have survived without [mentor], she's become a really good friend.

In addition, as was mentioned earlier, the parent knew that the mentor had been through similar experiences with her children:

> ...she's been through the same, that's important, that she's been there, that was really important, she knew what I was going through.

Overall, this mentee was extremely positive about the mentoring project. She felt the service should be more widely used, as it could benefit many more parents. As she said:

> ...a damned good scheme I think. I'd really hit rock bottom and [the mentor] helped me to keep going.

> ...more people should be told, advertise it everywhere.

The mentee above was the only person who was interviewed who went through the formal mentoring scheme. In addition, however, there was some brief information provided to the evaluator by the users of the HOPE drop-in centre at the London site. The three parents who provided feedback were very positive about the HOPE drop-in. They were attending the service for a range of reasons, but mainly because of a range of difficulties in their parenting – rude and abusive children, young people refusing to attend school and custody issues that were affecting them and their children's behaviour. All three parents had visited the drop-in before, and felt it provided them with useful information and support. As these parents said:

> ...just to chat is important, you know, people listen...

> Being a parent on my own, you know, it's hard, and can be lonely and here, like, I just don't feel so alone.

All three hoped that the drop-in would continue, and felt they would recommend it to other parents.

Conclusions and recommendations

This section summarises the main learning points that came out of the project, as follows:

- development of projects and training of mentors
- advertising and recruiting of mentees
- mentor–mentee relationships and supervision
- practical aspects
- funding issues
- being part of a broader programme.

Development of projects and training of mentors

- Developing a parent mentoring project takes considerable time. This must be built into planning. In particular, recruiting and training mentors, and identifying sources of mentees, takes a long time.

- A flexible and adaptable approach is needed to run a parent mentoring project. If one aspect does not work, it is important to persevere and try something else.

- It can take a very long time for CRB checks to be completed. It is important to start the application process as early as possible, and have a fallback plan for what the mentors can do if the CRB result is delayed.

- It is important to acknowledge that people become mentors for a variety of different reasons and advertising and recruitment must reflect this. Many parents will be motivated by wanting to 'give something back' and make a difference. However, others will also be attracted by gaining skills (and possibly qualifications) and having enhanced career prospects. It is important to 'sell' all the benefits of being a mentor.

- Advertising materials, fliers and the like are best produced by the mentors themselves. They have already joined a parenting course, and been trained as a mentor, and so know what is attractive to parents.

- It is important to have a well-thought-through training programme for the mentors, which includes social activities and fun in the training. One option for the future is to produce a training pack for this, to prevent the reinventing of the wheel.

Advertising and recruiting of mentees

- If schools are used as a way of recruiting mentees, a good link with the school or a 'champion' in the school is essential. This person needs to build relationships with parents and encourage mentees to come forward.

- It is difficult to recruit male mentors. One way of addressing this is to invite mixed-sex couples to take part, or to target mentoring programmes at fathers only.

- Mentoring should not be used for parents with a wide range of difficulties or severe problems, where statutory intervention is more appropriate. A clear finding was that whilst mentoring should not be used *in place of* statutory services, it could be used *in conjunction with* them. Clear guidelines and boundaries are needed so that inappropriate referrals are not made.

- Thought needs to be given to the format of the support provided, i.e. whether face to face or over the telephone. It was not clear from this project whether one format worked better than the other. However, it is important for future projects to consider the pros and cons of each method for the mentors that they are working with.

- An informal mentoring model could also work well – as has been described, many of the mentors became known in their workplaces as people who could listen and give advice about parenting. This model could be formalised – for example so that parents are trained as mentors not to 'work' in a specific setting, but as the need arises in their social/work lives.

Mentor–mentee relationships and supervision

- As stated above, it is important to give consideration to the mode of support provided, i.e. whether it is face to face or over the telephone. It may be appropriate for future projects to offer a mixture of these methods, depending on the parents involved and their circumstances.

- It was suggested by several workers in the project that some parents, particularly disadvantaged parents, might distrust other parents or be sceptical of what they can provide. These parents might be particularly anxious about confidentiality. It is important to work with mentors and potential mentees to address these issues.

- Several of the workers, and the mentors, in this project raised issues about professional boundaries. For example, to what extent should workers expect mentors to behave in certain 'professional' ways – for example not using swear words, smoking in front of service users, or using unacceptable language such as 'half caste'? These issues must be agreed and become part of written guidelines.

- Boundaries are very important in working with parents – where certain issues arise (for example child protection issues), there must be clear boundaries and guidelines in relation to what mentors can and cannot do.

Practical aspects

- If mentors are doing telephone interviewing, there should be dedicated telephones for this. This will ensure that both mentors and mentees do not have to use their own telephones, and thus keep boundaries appropriate. It may be possible to secure some sponsorship for this.

- The word 'mentor' was not always used across the three sites in this project. This was because some people did not feel comfortable with the term and felt it implied 'expert'. Thus, some sites used the word 'volunteer' instead.

Funding issues

- The funding provided in this pilot project was relatively small. This money was used (at all three sites) mainly for practical expenses, such as travel costs, training materials, office expenses and mobile phones. Thus, no staff time was covered by these expenses – any future projects need to address this issue.

- Additional funding needs to be secured where possible, as most of the projects cost more to run than was originally estimated.

Being part of a broader programme

- The three sites involved in the parent mentoring programme each said that they benefited from being part of a broader programme. This helped in terms of learning from others and having 'milestones' to reach in the project.

- Being part of a broader programme can help organisations to develop useful guidelines for parent mentoring projects. For example, projects in this pilot study were keen to obtain guidelines for doing telephone work and counselling. This could be put together by a project coordinator.

Learning for practitioners

- Whilst mentoring is widely used in youth projects, parent-to-parent mentoring has rarely been trialled.

- Whilst parent mentoring has considerable potential, there are many difficulties and hurdles to be overcome for it to work effectively.

- The issues raised in this chapter indicate those areas that need addressing in order for parent mentoring to work effectively.

- Parent mentoring is a flexible form of parent support that can be used in a variety of ways such as 'drop-in' settings.

Part 4
Conclusions

12 Parenting young people: research, policy and practice

Debi Roker and John Coleman

The chapters in this book have addressed some key questions in relation to supporting the parents of young people. As we proposed in the introduction to the book, the field of parenting support has expanded rapidly in recent years. From relatively little recognition of the needs of parents of young people in the early 1990s, there is now both increased recognition and a wide range of policy and practice initiatives underway. Despite these developments, however, there is still relatively little research into both some of the fundamental questions in the area and the effectiveness of different activities and interventions. The Trust for the Study of Adolescence's (TSA's) research, described in this volume, aimed to fill some of these knowledge gaps.

This final chapter of the book aims to identify some of the key issues that have emerged and offer some general conclusions about working with the parents of young people. The chapters have covered a diverse range of topics. These include: What is monitoring and supervision in families? How do parents view family communication about alcohol? How can young people be involved in parenting programmes? What do parents think of newsletters, or parent mentoring, as forms of information and support? Each chapter has aimed to identify the practical and applied uses of the research described. In doing so, a number of common themes, issues and questions can be identified. These are detailed below, in the following main sections:

- the range of ways in which information, advice and support can be provided

- the nature of 'extended' parenting

- the importance of reviewing service provision in different areas of parent support

- the balance between 'targeted' and 'general' support for the parents of young people

- the value of research into 'key' topics in parenting

- evaluation of innovative projects

- networking and professional development for practitioners

- using research in policy and practice

- issues of power and responsibility in parenting young people

- the 'old' and the 'new' in parenting support.

The range of ways in which information, advice and support can be provided

A number of the chapters explored innovative ways in which information and advice can be offered to parents. Crucially, each included an evaluation, in order to provide an evidence base for the effectiveness of different forms of support. Where possible, parents' views of the different types of support have been included. The chapter by Roker and Shepherd (Chapter 8), for example, explored the use of *newsletters* as a form of advice and support. In general, the parents and practitioners involved in both the 'general' and 'community' newsletters projects were extremely positive. Parents in particular liked the user-friendly 'magazine' style, and the fact that newsletters could be shared between friends and family and used to promote discussion with children and young people. Interestingly, some commentators in the field of parenting support describe written materials as old-fashioned and out of date. Clearly, however, many parents value this form of support. Newsletters are also a versatile and adaptable form of information and support, as TSA's move from producing 'general' to 'specialist' newsletters for parents with particular needs shows well. The chapter that described the needs of parents during the move to secondary school (Chapter 5) also confirmed this view – many parents wanted information about the transition in written form. (The issue of 'old' and 'new' technologies in parenting support is returned to later in this chapter.)

Other chapters in the book described different methods, and settings, for providing information and support to the parents of young people. The chapter by Roker and Richardson Foster (Chapter 7) described two interventions based in *schools*, offering three different types of support – materials, group-based courses and a Parent Adviser. As the results of the evaluations showed, large numbers of parents used the services. This was particularly the case at the school in the more disadvantaged area, where parents were regularly asking school staff for help and support in relation to their parenting. One of the advantages of offering parents support via schools is that the services provided are universal. No parent is stigmatised or made to feel they are being singled out for help. The development of extended schools will make it all the more important that we understand how schools can best provide information and advice to the parents in their community.

In considering the range of settings in which parenting support can be provided, a chapter by Roker considered the use of *websites* (Chapter 9). As stated in that chapter, despite the rapid rise in the number of websites providing information and support to parents, there has been little opportunity to review and assess this provision. As the results of the chapter show, many parents felt frustrated in their attempts to use websites in relation to parenting. However, when parents did locate useful and relevant sites, they were very impressed by the range and diversity of the information available. Such reviews need to be undertaken regularly, so that website provision matches parents' needs and expectations.

The three chapters mentioned above are examples of just three settings for providing advice and support to parents of young people – using newsletters, providing support in schools and via websites. There are many other forms and settings for support – some related issues are explored below.

The nature of 'extended' parenting

A number of the chapters in the book have added to our knowledge about who is involved in the parenting task, in relation to young people. The chapter by Roker and Stace (Chapter 2), for example, explored how parents and young people understood monitoring and supervision and how this was negotiated and contested within families. One of the key findings from this study was that few parents felt that they monitored and supervised young people alone. Many described how neighbours, friends, family and people in the community were all involved in monitoring and supervising their children. They described how all these groups 'kept an eye' on their children whilst they were in their care, or if they saw them around in the local community. Many parents also described how they expected the parents of their children's friends to monitor and supervise them when they were in their homes. Few of the parents, therefore, saw their parenting as something that was done in isolation.

This notion of 'extended' parenting was most graphically illustrated by Stace and Lowe in Chapter 3. These authors demonstrate very clearly the range of people who are often involved in bringing up children and young people – in the case of young people in foster care, this includes birth parents, foster parents and social workers, amongst others. The notion of 'team' or 'corporate' parenting is an important one and is a clear reminder that few children or young people are brought up in isolation. 'Extended' or 'team' parenting is a useful topic for future research.

The importance of reviewing service provision in different areas of parent support

Chapter 6 described a UK-wide review of transition to secondary school support for children and parents. This project revealed a number of important findings, including the range and nature of projects available, the rapid increase in provision and the precarious funding situation of many projects. This review is a good example of the value of monitoring the current situation in diverse areas of parenting support. The authors are aware that the information from this review has been used in many different ways by both practitioners and policy-makers. Thus, the results have been used:

- by practitioners to support their applications for project and organisational funding

- by practitioners and policy-makers to support awareness raising and campaigns, in relation to the importance of transition support

- by policy-makers when talking about the patchy nature of transition support, both for children and in particular for parents.

It is considered that a number of other areas in relation to parenting support would benefit from such a review. These areas include the use of Parenting Orders, the range of options available for work with this group of parents, the development of new materials for parenting programmes, advances in work with fathers and work with special groups of parents such as those with a disability or those with mental health problems.

The balance between 'targeted' and 'general' support for the parents of young people

One of the key issues that has emerged in this book relates to whether support for parents is offered on a universal or a targeted basis. This is a long-standing issue in the field of parenting support and many practitioners and policy-makers have very strong views about it. A number of interesting observations about this topic can be made from the chapters in the present book. The 'newsletters' project (in Chapter 8) is a good example of work that looked at both sides of this issue. The first project described in this chapter produced 'general' newsletters, which aimed to be of use to all the 4000 or so parents in the four schools involved in the pilot. The majority of the parents were generally very positive about the newsletters and found things of interest and value in them.

The advantages of distributing the newsletters to everyone at the schools involved was that no one was singled out for special treatment – the newsletters were promoted as being for everyone. This approach clearly has advantages. However, it also has disadvantages, notably that people with very specific needs (such as lone parents, parents from different cultural backgrounds, or parents of children with special needs) do not receive the targeted support that they need.

The 'community' newsletter described in the same chapter described TSA's second project, which aimed to provide specialist, targeted support to parents with particular needs, also demonstrated the value of this approach. Parents in all of the community groups were extremely positive about the ways in which the newsletters provided help and support in relation to their situations. These two projects, therefore, suggest that both universal and targeted approaches to parenting support have value. Other chapters in the book also demonstrate the value of both approaches – for example in the chapter on the use of websites as a form of support (Chapter 9), some parents really valued the 'general' support offered on websites provided by organisations such as Parentline Plus and the National Family and Parenting Institute. However, they also valued the information and support provided on particular topics (such as drug use, disabilities, dealing with divorce, etc.). It is unlikely, therefore, that one or the other approach alone would provide the information, advice and support that the parents of young people need.

The value of research into 'key' topics in parenting

In the field of research, there is often a debate about the value of 'basic' or theoretical research, compared to applied or evaluation research. The distinction between these two types of research can be illustrated by the chapters in this book. Examples of research into key concepts in parenting are demonstrated by the chapter by Roker and Stace into monitoring and supervision in families (Chapter 2), and the chapter by Cox and colleagues into family communication about alcohol in families (Chapter 4). Neither of these studies focused on interventions of particular projects or activities, but rather on understanding fundamental concepts in parenting and family relationships.

We consider that such research is extremely important, in that it sheds light on some of the key ideas and relationships that impact on parenting policy and practice. This information can then be used to inform the support offered to parents and the policies that are implemented in the area. Indeed, both of the studies above are already being used to inform policy and practice, via the development of training materials for practitioners and materials for parents. It is, however, increasingly difficult to get funding for such 'basic' and more theoretical research. Few funders are providing grants for such research, with the Joseph Rowntree Foundation being a notable exception. We feel strongly that future research in relation to parenting young people must focus both on understanding key concepts and ideas and on the evaluation of new interventions and projects.

Evaluation of innovative projects

Many of the chapters in this book illustrate how evaluation has been included as an important feature of the intervention or project. As is generally recognised today, evaluation must play a role in the development of practice, yet there remain serious limitations with much evaluation. There are now many new initiatives and activities being undertaken by practitioners in a range of settings. All of these aim to provide information, advice and support to parents in one way or another. It has to be said, however, that the evaluation of such projects is patchy. As the chapter by Roker and Shepherd demonstrates (in relation to the UK-wide review of transition projects, Chapter 6) much innovative work is being undertaken without detailed evaluation. As a result, we have little information about effectiveness and little opportunity of sharing learning and good practice that comes out of these projects.

It is important here to note that there are many different types of evaluation, not all of them appropriate or indeed possible to use in the contexts described in this book. The simplest distinction to make is that between process and outcome evaluation. With the latter it would be expected that studies would be of a longer duration than is normally the case in the UK, requiring research that continues after the conclusion of the intervention process. Outcomes of interest might include a reduction in antisocial behaviour, improved school performance or attendance and lower levels of risk behaviour such as the use of illegal substances. Studies looking at such outcomes are common in the US and in Australia, but are rare in the UK, primarily because of a lack of funding for such work. As a consequence, what is most often seen in the UK is what is known as process evaluation. This evaluation usually lasts the length of the intervention programme, or ends shortly after the completion of the programme. It concerns itself with the gathering of information on topics such as the attitudes and knowledge of parents, their satisfaction with the intervention, their general well-being or self-esteem, and attendance levels of clients on parenting programmes. This type of evaluation is extremely useful, as has been described above, yet it is important to note that the development of evidence-based practice in the UK is most often based on process rather than outcome evaluation, as is the case in other countries. More research that combines process and outcome evaluation is needed.

The authors consider that more funding and resources need to be dedicated to providing both process and outcome evaluation of innovative work in the UK. In the present book we mainly document examples of process evaluation, and the value of this is demonstrated in many of the chapters. For example the evaluation of the 'parent mentors' scheme showed the difficulties involved in running a parent-to-parent mentoring service (Chapter 11). However, it also enabled the recording of the good practice and learning that came out of this pilot project, which is now being used by others who are involved in setting up such schemes. Similarly, the evaluation of the newsletters project (Chapter 8), and the school-based support projects (Chapter 7) meant that key lessons for the future could be learnt from these innovative projects. Although these projects were both undertaken a few years ago, the results of the two evaluations are still being regularly used to inform new work, and by practitioners and policy-makers working in the field of parent support.

Networking and professional development for practitioners

One of the issues that has emerged in the chapters has been how practitioners working with parents develop their knowledge and skills and hear about good and promising practice. The TSA has come across this issue in a range of its work, and is involved in a number of practice development projects. Many of the chapters in this book demonstrate how important it is to support those who work with parents to share knowledge and develop their skills.

In the UK-wide review (Chapter 6) for example, many of the project workers involved were aware that they often 'reinvented the wheel' in setting up projects to support children and parents. Most practitioners, understandably, find it frustrating that there are few networks available to share learning and good practice with others working in the same field. It is essential, therefore, that more such networks are established. The TSA has taken steps to address this issue in its work. One of its Department for Education and Skills-funded projects is focusing on practitioners who work to support parents of 8- to 11-year-olds, particularly around the transition to secondary school. One aspect of this project is an email 'newsletter', circulated free to people working in this field every 6 to 8 weeks. The newsletter contains relevant research, materials, training events, conferences, etc. and has a 'noticeboard' section where practitioners can share and ask for information. This method of networking and professional development is considered to be a good model for future work to support practitioners. Clearly, however, more is needed, and the government will need to take responsibility for much of this. The establishment of the Children's Workforce Development Council is considered to be a positive step forward in this respect.

Using research in policy and practice

A key theme of this book, and the individual chapters within it, is the use of research to inform and support policy and practice in relation to the parenting of young people. As an example, one of the aspects that characterises all the chapters in the book is the collection and use of parents' real-life experiences in relation to parenting. This is considered particularly important and these case studies, quotes and comments can be used in a variety of ways by practitioners. The use of qualitative material reflecting the views of parents is an extremely powerful way of getting messages across, of prompting discussion and debate and of illustrating the realities of life for parents and families today.

The information from the chapters in the book is being used in a wide range of ways by TSA, in order to support practice and work with parents. A few examples demonstrate this well. The chapter by Stace and Lowe (Chapter 3), for example, describes their important research into 'team' parenting of young people in foster care. This research is currently being used to develop training materials to support both foster carers and the practitioners who work with them. Again, the real-life experiences of young people in foster care and of foster carers will bring this material to life. Similarly, the chapter on monitoring and supervision (Chapter 2) has been used to produce a 'Toolkit' of groupwork activities and other material for practitioners to use in their work with parents. Very positive feedback has been received about these materials, in particular that hearing directly from young people and parents makes the issues feel real and reassures parents that other people experience the same issues and difficulties that they do. Similarly, the chapter on general and community newsletters (Chapter 8) included many quotes and examples from parents and the evaluation showed how other parents found these both interesting, reassuring and useful to discuss with other family members and young people. The value of 'real-life' quotes and case studies should not be underestimated in work with the parents of young people.

Issues of power and responsibility in parenting young people

In the introductory chapter to this volume, we highlighted the tensions that are inherent in relation to responsibility for young people's behaviour and actions. We described, for example, how young people can receive confidential health advice and information without their parents' knowledge, but that parents remain legally responsible for school attendance as well as for any criminal behaviour of a young person under the age of 18. Sanctions, in the form of Parenting Orders, can be imposed if parents are seen to 'shirk' their responsibilities for their children's behaviour.

The chapters in this book demonstrate some of these tensions and difficulties in practice. The chapter on monitoring and supervision (Chapter 2), for example, shows how many parents struggled with the issues of parent–child relationships, monitoring, negotiation and young people's growing independence. Most parents struggled with balancing their own desire to monitor their children's whereabouts and activities, as a way of protecting them, with the inevitable need to allow young people to develop their own autonomy and independence. Crucially, many of the parents in this study also described how they cannot know '100 per cent of the time' where their children are and what they are doing. Similarly, the chapter by Cox *et al.* in relation to young people and alcohol (Chapter 4), demonstrates many parents' views that they have little control over many aspects of their children's lives. Both these studies highlight the difficulty, described in the introductory chapter, of making parents legally responsible for their children's school attendance or involvement in criminal behaviour.

Other chapters in the book demonstrate the complexity of the parent–young person relationship. The chapter by Hoskin and Lindfield (Chapter 10), for example, describes the issues involved in working with both parents and young people in parenting programmes. The issues involved in this type of initiative are considerable. However, what this chapter does demonstrate is that both parents and young people are equal and active participants in the parent–young person relationship. Whilst much parenting literature has historically viewed young people as passive recipients of parental control and management, recent research shows that young people must be seen as active participants in family relationships.

The 'old' and the 'new' in parenting support

One of the interesting issues that has emerged in the collection of chapters in this book has been the issue of 'old' and 'new' forms of parenting support. By 'old', we mean formats such as newsletters, leaflets and (arguably) group-based programmes. By 'new', we mean those characterised in particular by new technologies, including telephone helplines, websites, interactive CDs and email.

Many commentators, and some policy initiatives, suggest that new technologies should be the focus of much of the support that is offered to parents in the future. However, many of the chapters in this book do not support this proposal. Certainly, some chapters do suggest that newer forms of support can be useful for parents – for example Roker's chapter on information and support via websites shows how useful these formats can be (Chapter 9). However, the chapters also show that the 'older' formats, involving parents talking to and supporting each other, written materials such as newsletters etc., can be very useful. This finding is reflected in the chapters describing TSA's school-based projects (Chapter 7), the parent mentors chapter (Chapter 11) and the newsletter chapter (Chapter 8). We can conclude, therefore, that a balance of types of support is critical, as no one approach is going to suit every parent.

Conclusions

The world of parenting is in a period of rapid change. This applies to all parenting work, but is especially true for parents of young people. In the course of this book we have demonstrated some of the ways in which this change is evident in the contexts of research, policy and practice. We believe that there is a clear need for research that will inform the processes of change and will assist policy-makers as well as practitioners in the developments that are taking place in relation to supporting parents of young people.

In this book there is a wide range of examples of innovative work designed to do precisely this. Either through basic research, such as that on monitoring and supervision, or through studies of new types of intervention, such as that on the use of newsletters, we have set out the findings of studies that can highlight possible new directions. Furthermore, we believe that in these pages are to be found a multitude of examples of lessons that can be applied to practice. How projects and interventions have worked or not worked is essential information if the field is to progress. A good example of this point is to be found in the chapter on parent mentoring (Chapter 11). 'What a good idea,' many might say. Yet, as can be seen from the findings of the study reported here, all is not as simple as it might at first appear. The chapter on the use of websites also falls into this category (Chapter 9). With so many organisations using websites to get information to parents, the conclusions to be drawn from this chapter should be invaluable for all who hope to use new technology in their work with parents.

If it achieves anything, the learning to be found in this book should prevent practitioners experiencing a continual 'reinvention of the wheel'. The field of parenting is at an exciting stage of growth and development. We hope that the chapters will serve as a contribution towards better policy formulation and more effective practice in the future. Through our work at TSA we seek to improve the lives of young people and their families. We have had a long-standing commitment to supporting parents of young people and the work documented in this book reflects that commitment.

Subject index

Author index